W9-BAJ-706

Rewriting the Rules of the American Economy

Also by Joseph E. Stiglitz

The Great Divide:
Unequal Societies and What We Can Do About Them

Creating a Learning Society:
A New Approach to Growth, Development,
and Social Progress (with Bruce C. Greenwald)

The Price of Inequality:
How Today's Divided Society Endangers Our Future

Freefall:
America, Free Markets, and the Sinking of the World Economy

The Three Trillion Dollar War:
The True Cost of the Iraq Conflict (with Linda J. Bilmes)

Making Globalization Work

Fair Trade for All:
How Trade Can Promote Development (with Andrew Charlton)

The Roaring Nineties:
A New History of the World's Most Prosperous Decade

Globalization and Its Discontents

Rewriting the Rules of the American Economy

AN AGENDA FOR GROWTH AND SHARED PROSPERITY

JOSEPH E. STIGLITZ

with Nell Abernathy, Adam Hersh,
Susan Holmberg, and Mike Konczal

A Roosevelt Institute book

W. W. NORTON & COMPANY
Independent Publishers Since 1923
New York • London

For information about permission to reproduce selections from this book,
write to Permissions, W. W. Norton & Company, Inc.,
500 Fifth Avenue, New York, NY 10110

For information about special discounts for bulk purchases, please contact
W. W. Norton Special Sales at specialsales@wwnorton.com or 800-233-4830

Book design by Ellen Cipriano Design
Production manager: Julia Druskin

ISBN: 978-0-393-25405-1
        978-0-393-35312-9 (pbk.)

W. W. Norton & Company, Inc.
500 Fifth Avenue, New York, N.Y. 10110
www.wwnorton.com

W. W. Norton & Company Ltd.
Castle House, 75/76 Wells Street, London W1T 3QT

1 2 3 4 5 6 7 8 9 0

CONTENTS

PREFACE

The American economy—and its discontents

Rewriting the Rules comes at a watershed political moment. Americans are anxious and angry, and rightfully so. This is, of course, a book about economics, but it is really about people.

The vast majority of Americans—not just the poor—are deeply worried about the very basics: getting their kids a decent education, bringing home a paycheck that can put food on the table or pay the bills, saving enough so that one day they can retire. In the 2008 crisis and the deep recession that followed, more than 10 million families lost their homes or entered foreclosure, and 8.7 million workers lost their jobs. Even now, those with a home are worried about keeping it, and many displaced workers have either permanently dropped out of the workforce or taken low-skill jobs for less pay.

However, as this book will show, these economic troubles are not a recent phenomenon, and not only attributable to the crisis. Decades of meager pay have eroded not just economic security but also hope for a better future. For too many Americans, achieving or maintaining a middle-class lifestyle seems increasingly out of reach. They hear about economic "growth" and "recovery" on the news but don't see that translated into steady income or growing paychecks. Those at the top have more than recovered what they lost in the crisis as the stock market has soared. But not so the rest, who saw what little wealth they had wiped out. Ninety-one percent of all increases in income from 2009 to 2012 went to the wealthiest 1 percent of Americans—the epitome of unequal growth.

Some commentators point to other signs of recovery, especially in the job market. But despite a headline unemployment rate of 5.3 percent, millions remain trapped in disguised unemployment and part-time employment. The workforce participation rate has fallen to levels that predate women's widespread entry into the labor market in the late 1970s. The unemployment rate including those working part time involuntarily and those who are marginally attached—meaning they want a job but are not actively looking for work—is over 10 percent. In communities of color, rates are even higher, with unemployment among African-Americans double that of whites—as has been true for half a century.

Across every political divide, across every generational divide, and across our anguished racial divide, the American people are hungry for a new direction and for solutions that will create a path to a new and widely shared prosperity. Politicians in both parties now struggle to speak the language of inequality, trying to find ways to connect to the electorate's anxiety. The 99 percent and the 1 percent have become part of the national dialogue. But no national leader has yet figured out how to explain, forthrightly and clearly, how the U.S. has become a nation—with so much talent and such a track record of growth and innovation—now mired in such chronic suffering. Nor has anyone laid out a clear, comprehensive plan to lead the country out of the morass.

It is in this moment that we offer a simple idea: we can rewrite the rules of the American economy so they work better—not just for the wealthy, but for everyone.

Our Answer: Rewriting the Rules

This book has been written to help explain what's wrong with the economy and how to fix it. It lays out a broad agenda for how we can rewrite the rules of the 21st century economy to achieve shared prosperity, with enough detail to show what needs to be done and to provide confidence that—if there is the political will—it *can* be done.

This book was originally released as a report through the Roosevelt Institute, and was intended primarily for political decision-makers. But it struck a nerve far beyond that group. *The*

New York Times called it "an aggressive blueprint for rewriting 35 years of policies that . . . have led to a vast concentration of wealth among the richest Americans and an increasingly squeezed middle class." *Time* magazine said *Rewriting the Rules* revealed a "secret truth" about inequality. The Ford Foundation called the report a "landmark." Of course, politicians listened, too. Senator Elizabeth Warren lauded the report as "groundbreaking." Advocates, labor leaders, members of Congress, and presidential candidates called, requesting briefings and discussions and further explications of "the rules." Importantly, they saw the report as a call to action: what could we do, specifically, now, to begin to create a stronger economy?

What We Thought We Knew about Economics Was Wrong—and Why That's a Good Thing

The core message here is simple: The American economy is not out of balance because of the natural laws of economics. Today's inequality is not the result of the inevitable evolution of capitalism. Instead, the rules that govern the economy got us here. And we can change those rules using what we have learned in economics and what we know about the people who make the rules and how they are chosen. Best of all, changing the rules to promote economic stability for American families will actually be good for the economy.

The rules shaping our current economy were informed by an economic orthodoxy that we now know is incorrect and outdated. "Supply-side" economics posited that constraints imposed by regulations and disincentives imposed by taxes and a generous welfare system were limiting growth—a sharp break from earlier decades, when Keynesian economists emphasized insufficient demand as the limiting factor. Supply-side ideas led not only to deregulation and lower tax rates on top incomes, but also to cuts to social welfare programs and public investments. The results are now in: We cut top tax rates and repealed regulations, but the benefits didn't "trickle down" to everyone else. These policies increased wealth for the largest corporations and the richest Americans, increased economic inequality, and failed to produce the economic growth that adherents promised.

There has been a radical shift in economic theory since the middle of the 20th century, and a raft of new evidence allows us to better understand the strengths and limits of markets. The evidence shows that markets do not exist in a vacuum: they are shaped by our legal system and our political institutions. It also tells us that we can improve economic performance and reduce inequality at the same time. Put simply: the notion that we have to choose between economic growth and shared prosperity for many more Americans is false.

This is good news. Inequality—at the level and of the type that we see today—is a choice. When the rules no longer work, it's time to rewrite them.

The Role of Political Movements, Present and Past

The demand for real change is growing. This is both because of what Americans see and feel now, and what they sense is coming just around the corner.

Lackluster economic performance over many decades has moved economic concerns from the fringe to the very center of our political debate. Wages for most Americans are stagnant, but worker productivity continues to grow; the disparity between the two is unprecedented. At the top, though, CEO and bankers' incomes soar—with no concomitant improvement in the performance of the firms for which they are responsible. Although more flexible labor markets were supposed to bring about more job growth, this hasn't panned out, as the country faces a deficit of some three million jobs needed to reach pre-recession employment levels and absorb those who have joined the potential workforce. Eighty percent of the job growth we do see is in low-wage service and retail employment. This combination of growth for the very wealthy and economic stasis and anxiety for the rest of Americans is politically volatile.

Whereas the status quo is unsustainable, the future is no less daunting. Americans know that the economy is changing at its core. We are in a time of fundamental economic disruption. The resulting transformation of our economy—including changes in technology and globalization—holds both peril and promise. More and more people piece together a living as "micro-earners," working through a variety of platforms to offer rides or rooms or services—from cleaning to computer programming. The sharing economy may bring great freedom and flexibility, but certainly requires that we update a legal framework forged three-quarters of a century ago, when the National Labor Relations Act and the labor regulations that followed assumed a more sustained employer relationship and a narrower definition of what it means to be a worker.

Most Americans do not need economists to tell them that the changes and challenges we face demand comprehensive solutions. Piecemeal proposals that tinker at the margins of our current economic structure will not be sufficient to get our economy back on track. Indeed, it is very clear to the American public that the economy is not working. According to recent polling, nearly two-thirds of Americans—Republicans, Democrats, and independents—believe the gap between rich and poor must be addressed. We see an increasingly powerful set of social and political movements responding to these issues, from the Occupy movement and its successors, which focused in large part on the abuses of the financial sector, to the advocates fighting for wage increases, racial justice, college affordability, and housing finance. They are all expressing real and deep needs and demanding action.

This book focuses on the U.S., but what has happened here has also occurred in many other countries around the world. The international rules of the game have also been changed, often under the influence of the same misguided economic theories, reflecting the same ideologies and similar economic interests. In some cases, America has been seen as a role model; in others, it has used its influence at the World Bank, the IMF, the WTO, the G-20, and in other international settings to force the kind of changes that led to more inequality and poorer economic performance onto other countries.

The Window of Opportunity

At this time of widespread calls for change, *Rewriting the Rules* provides an interpretation of *why* our economy has been failing, and, on the basis of that analysis, a set of prescriptions that go well beyond tinkering at the edges. The slowing of our economy and the increase in inequality are two sides of the same coin. Changes instituted over the last thirty years have led to an increase in short-sighted behavior, with less spending on the kinds of long-term investments, including investments in people, that would generate high rates of sustainable growth. This short-term behavior has created an unstable economy, and we are still suffering from the fallout of the last major crisis.

We have created a so-called market economy that is rife with distortions, which enrich the top and stifle long-term growth. Creating shared prosperity is not just a matter of *redistribution*— redistributing after-market income through taxes and transfers— though that is very important. We must also increase wages, well-being, and ultimately economic and political power for the majority of Americans. Based on this set of observations, *Rewriting the Rules* suggests a comprehensive menu of answers, demonstrating that, in fact, there is something—in fact, many things—we can do to fight inequality *at the source*, which would at the same time create a more stable and faster-growing economy.

In today's gridlocked political environment, this might sound like an impossible task. But we can take inspiration from the past. The Progressive movement at the turn of the 20th century sought to protect and ultimately politically engage all Americans, including working people, as the American economy shifted radically away from the farm and agriculture to industry and factory jobs. These ideas culminated in real change. Theodore Roosevelt, realizing that concentrations of economic power would lead to concentrations of political power, sought to limit monopolies and trusts. Franklin Roosevelt's New Deal was, of course, a new set of policy ideas designed to fight the twin concentrations of economic and political power by remaking the social contract and improving the lot of average Americans in the then-new industrial economy; it was also a fundamental commitment to making those policy ideas a reality.

The New Deal was far from perfect, especially in its omissions of women and people of color, and we must work today to correct those shortfalls. But the arc from 1892 to 1938 shows that American politics can bring together outsider social movements and powerful political forces in the service of all citizens—to make profound structural change to the rules that govern our economy.

Today, we have the opportunity to see this happen again, and the obligation to push for it. These rules were decades in the making, and will take a long-term effort to fully rewrite. Middle- and working-class Americans have lived in fear for too long, but as Franklin Roosevelt told us, the only thing we have to fear is fear itself. *Rewriting the Rules* makes the case for pushing past that fear and taking control of our own economic future.

The wide coverage of the original Roosevelt Institute report suggests that many of those engaged in politics both in and outside of Washington are listening. Yet the analysis and arguments here demand more—they demand action. Will our political leadership have the courage to heed that call?

Rewriting the Rules was a team effort. A group of tremendous authors and researchers, including the Roosevelt Institute's Nell Abernathy, Adam Hersh, Susan Holmberg, and Mike Konczal, with extremely able research assistance from Eric Harris Bernstein, worked tirelessly to sift through massive quantities of data, historical analysis, and numerous policy solutions to craft a book that is both comprehensive and also pithy and persuasive. If *Rewriting the Rules* has succeeded in achieving this difficult balance, it is because of their acumen and very hard work.

Rewriting the Rules also would not have been written without the backing and faith of some prescient and ultimately optimistic individuals. We are grateful for the counsel and support from the

Ford Foundation, and especially from Darren Walker, Xavier de Souza Briggs, and Don Chen; and the MacArthur Foundation, with special thanks to Ianna Kachoris and Tara Magner. At just the right moment, Bernard L. Schwartz, a longtime visionary fighting for a stronger and healthier American economy, and his colleague Susan Torricelli stepped in with support, encouragement, and advice on how to make our arguments most effectively. And, of course, the Roosevelt Institute Board of Directors has provided regular and unflagging enthusiasm for our efforts to make academic evidence about what is happening to our economy more salient in the push and pull of today's politics. Anna Eleanor Roosevelt, in particular, has shown the same combination of political acumen, human compassion, and down-to-earth common sense that her grandparents showed in remaking the American economy and society more than eighty years ago.

We can only hope that we will show some of the same foresight, and some measure of the same success, today.

Joseph E. Stiglitz, chief economist, and
Felicia Wong, president and CEO
of the Roosevelt Institute

INTRODUCTION

The American economy no longer works for most Americans. We pride ourselves on being the land of opportunity and creating the first middle-class society, yet profound and largely overlooked changes have put the middle-class life increasingly out of reach for the majority of Americans. At the same time, we have enabled a small percentage of the population to take home the lion's share of economic gains.

The rapidly rising inequality in the United States over the past generation disturbs and baffles economists and politicians because it is unlike anything our economic models predict or our experience of the mid-20th century led us to expect.

What is causing this dysfunction? Economists have gone back to textbook models and examined reams of data to try to understand what is happening. Some point to technological change or globalization. Some posit that government has shackled the free enterprise system and hobbled business. Some say that our economy is simply rewarding the risk takers and job creators who have earned the riches coming their way. None of these arguments gets it right. This report, which sets out a new framework for understanding and addressing current economic trends, makes the following points:

- Skyrocketing incomes for the 1 percent and stagnating wages for everyone else are not independent phenomena, but rather two symptoms of an impaired economy that rewards gaming the system more than it does hard work and investment.
- As America has created more inequality than other advanced countries, opportunity has also been undermined. The American dream increasingly appears to be a myth, and this should not come as a surprise: economies with high levels of income inequality and wealth inequality tend to have low levels of equality of opportunity.
- The roots of this dysfunction lie deep in the rules and power dynamics that have prioritized corporate power and short-term gains at the expense of long-term innovation and growth.
- The outcomes shaped by these rules and power dynamics do not make the economy stronger; indeed, many make it weaker.
- A minimalist agenda that treats only the worst con-

sequences of inequality will not rewrite the rules and restructure the power dynamics that are driving stagnating wages and sputtering growth.

■ We can rewrite the rules that shape our economy to improve prospects for more Americans while also enhancing economic performance.

■ The effects of the growth of inequality over the past third of a century won't be undone overnight, and there are no silver bullets. However, there are policies that can once again put the sought-after but increasingly unattainable middle-class lifestyle within the grasp of most Americans.

With these points in mind, we need to think through what the government does and does not do, with a renewed focus on how each affects inequality. Instead of taking a minimalist approach, we have to tackle the rules and power dynamics that shape our daily lives.

We must understand that reducing inequality is not just a matter of *redistribution*. Economic policies affect the distribution of income both before and after taxes and transfers. The tax system, for instance, may encourage some inequality-generating activities at the expense of others. As we shall see, this is not just a theoretical possibility; it describes what has happened in the United States.

In traditional analyses based on models of perfect markets, we often assume away the rules of the game. It is as if markets

Rules include all the regulatory and legal frameworks and social norms that structure how the economy works. These include rules affecting property rights, the enforcement of contracts, the formation and behavior and responsibilities of businesses, relations between workers and their employers, and obligations and protections for borrowers and lenders and buyers and sellers in financial markets. They also include rules and institutions governing key aspects of public policymaking—taxes, public spending, and monetary policy. And they include the combination of written and unwritten rules that create a structural basis for discrimination that systematically excludes broad segments of the population—namely women and people of color—from social and economic opportunity.[1]

existed in a vacuum, structured by some natural law, and all that the economist needs to do to understand changes in the economy is to study the shapes of the demand and supply curves and the forces determining their shifts over time.

But few markets are perfectly competitive; therefore outcomes depend in part on market power, and rules affect this power. Bargaining power, for instance, determines who benefits the most from labor negotiations, and that power is affected by the strength of unions, the legal and economic environment, and how globalization is structured. In markets with imperfect competition, firms have their own form of market power: the power to set prices. Likewise, the political power of various groups determines their ability to have the rules of the market written and enforced in their favor.

Our challenge, then, is to rewrite the rules to work for everyone. To do so, we must re-learn what we thought we knew about how modern economies work. We must also devise new policies to eliminate the inefficiencies and conflicts of interest that pervade our financial sector, our corporate rules, our macroeconomic, monetary, tax, expenditure, and competition policies, our labor relations, and our political structures. It is important to engage all of these challenges simultaneously, since our economy is a system and these elements interact. This will not be easy; we must push to achieve these fundamental changes at a time when the American people have lost faith in their government's ability to act in service of the common good.

The problems we face today are in large part the result of economic decisions we made—or failed to make—beginning in the late 1970s. The changes occurring in our economy, politics, and society have been dramatic, and there is a corresponding sense of urgency in this report. We cannot afford to go forward with minor tweaks and hope that they do the trick. We know the answer: they will not, and the suffering that will occur in the meantime is unconscionable. And, as we explain, this is not just about the present, but the future. The policies of today are "baking in" the America of 2050: unless we change course, we will be a country with slower growth, ever more inequality, and ever less equality of opportunity.

Inequality has been a choice, and it is within our power to reverse it.

Market power

noun

1. The ability to set both the terms of market exchange and the rules that govern exchange.

What the Old Models Got Wrong

The economic experiences of the last 35 years have pulled the rug out from under many of our traditional conceptions of economic theory and the trajectory of economic growth. When President Kennedy said that "a rising tide lifts all boats," he gave voice to a theory of progress that had guided thinking in economics and policy for years.[2] In the 1950s Nobel laureate Simon Kuznets suggested that, while inequality would increase in the initial stages of any economy's development, it would eventually decrease as an economy became more advanced.[3] While Kuznets's observation accurately described the dramatic decrease in inequality for several decades after the start of World War II, history since the 1970s contradicts his hypothesis.* During the last few decades, the benefits of economic growth have dispro-

---

* Over the longer run, there could, of course, be either increases or decreases in the distribution of income as changes in the savings rate, population growth rate, and technology affect whether there is capital deepening (an increase in the ratio of capital to effective labor). However, as we argue, it is difficult for these factors to explain observed changes in inequality.

portionately gone to the top 20 percent of the population while the share of national income going to the bottom 99 percent has fallen.[4] Incomes, especially for men, have stagnated during this time.[5] More urgently, between 2010 and 2013, even as the economy was supposed to be in a recovery, median wages fell further.[6] We now know that developed economies can rise without lifting all boats.

Our economic world has been rocked as well by new understandings of the relationship between inequality and economic performance. In the past, this was typically viewed as a tradeoff: we could only have more equality at the cost of a reduction in economic performance. Arthur Okun, chairman of the Council of Economic Advisers under President Lyndon Johnson, once described the apparent inverse relationship between efficiency and equality as the "big tradeoff."[7] At that time the focus on achieving greater equality was redistribution (more progressive taxes and transfers). These, it was thought, would adversely affect incentives, and this would undermine economic performance. Thus, one could lessen the degree of inequality only by sacrificing economic performance.[8] But new evidence shows that nations can successfully combat inequality without harming, and perhaps even while promoting, economic performance.[9]

Since the late '70s, we have seen a decline in our growth rate, four significant economic downturns—including the worst since the Great Depression—and an increasing share of the limited growth that has occurred going to the top, with stagnant incomes for many and a hollowing out of the middle class. Evidently, trickle-down economics—increasing incomes at the top in the hope that everyone will benefit—has not worked. The new view is that trickle-up economics—building out the economy from the middle—is more likely to bring success; in other words, equality and economic performance are *complements*, not substitutes.

The demise of these tenets of conventional wisdom has profound consequences. It tells us that we cannot take shared growth for granted, and that we do not need to circumscribe our efforts to promote shared growth simply out of fear that such efforts will necessarily damage economic performance. Recent research has identified the many channels through which greater inequality hurts economic performance, and why it is that higher GDP growth does not necessarily benefit large swaths of the population.[10]

This new view emphasizes that policies that focus only on the symptoms of our dysfunctional economy—for instance, on remedying the worst extremes of inequality—will not change the way today's economy is structured nor tackle the reasons that our economy seems to generate more inequality than the economies of any other advanced countries. The experience of the last 35 years, across many nations, suggests that rules of finance, corporate governance, and international trade all can be rewritten to promote growth and shared prosperity rather than channel more wealth and opportunity toward those who already have the most.

Textbook models trying to explain inequality focus on a

simple theory: each individual receives returns commensurate with his or her social contributions. Differences in individuals' incomes are then related to differences in productivity, skills, and effort, and changes in the distribution are attributed, for instance, to changes in technology and to investments in human and physical capital. Following such an analysis, much of the wage inequality that emerged in the latter part of the 20th century was attributed to "skill-biased" technological change, the fact that changes in technology put a greater premium on certain skills, and that individuals with those skills did better than the rest. To the extent that these skills were acquired through education, over the long run, wage premium would induce more young people to acquire these highly valued skills, and as they did so, the premium would be reduced. The high level of the education premium reflected a mismatch between the needs of the new technologies and our labor force. These were important insights, and certain policies followed: providing a larger proportion of the population with these skills would reduce inequality.

But there are serious deficiencies and limitations in these theories, as we will explain in an appendix. Skill-biased technological change, for example, cannot explain why highly skilled workers have had to move into lower-skilled jobs. It cannot explain what has been happening to wages in the past decade—even skilled workers are not doing well. Nor can it explain the magnitude of the rise of pay at the top—including CEOs and those in the financial sector—or the yawning gap between the growth in productivity of workers as a whole and average wages.

Historically, wage and productivity growth moved in tandem, but this has not been true for the last third of a century.

Of course, inequality and how the overall gains from growth get distributed among individuals are complex phenomena caused by a number of factors. Technology, globalization, shifting demographics, and other major forces are important, and parsing out the relative contributions of different factors is not simple. But these forces are largely global in nature. If they are the primary drivers, all advanced countries should be similarly affected. But among advanced economy countries, the U.S. has the highest level of inequality, so the explanation for the outcomes we see cannot lie solely in global factors.[11] Moreover, not even the effects of global forces are out of our control. Their impact can be changed significantly by the policy decisions we make. Given the failings of the older models, we have an alternative explanation for the extreme inequality we see today.

An Emerging Approach: The Importance of Institutions and Correcting Structural Imbalance

Our institutionalist approach is based on two simple economic observations: rules matter and power matters. This approach began with a set of insights from academic research. Over the past four decades, economists have increasingly drawn attention to the many ways that the standard model, which assumes perfect information, perfect competition, perfect risk markets, and perfect rationality, fails to provide an accurate description of how various markets in our economy really work. Researchers including myself, George Akerloff, Michael Spence, Jean Tirole, Daniel Kahneman, Oliver Williamson, Douglas North, John Harsanyi, John Nash, Richard Selten, Elinor Ostrom, Rob Shiller, and others have won Nobel prizes for work on information asymmetries and imperfections, bargaining theory and imperfections of competition, behavioral economics, and institutional analysis. These works provide a whole new perspective on the functioning of labor, product, and financial markets, and essentially show that institutions and rules are required to force markets to behave competitively, for the benefit of all. And even when markets are competitive, there can be "market failures," important instances where government intervention is required to ensure efficient and socially desirable outcomes.

That theory has been substantiated by a number of real-life events. The economic crisis of 2008 and the Great Recession that followed demonstrated that the promise of a deregulated market economy was empty. Only through concerted government action, in the form of an $800 billion bailout, were the banks and the market sustained.[12] Further, saving the financial system did not trickle down to ordinary mortgage holders or average workers, who lost over 4 million homes and whose real median income declined nearly 8 percent between 2007 and 2013.[13]

In sum, while both the traditional and institutionalist economic approaches explain some of what has been going on, the latter theory, which focuses on structural factors, is increasingly compelling.

Wealth and Inequality

Economists are developing a new set of theories in an effort to explain the profound imbalance we see in today's economy, in particular the rise in wealth relative to income. In *Capital in the 21st Century*, Thomas Piketty argues that r>g—meaning the return to capital is greater than the growth rate of the overall economy—and that wealth grows faster than income as a result. This means that, if the return to capital does not decline (and he argues that it has not), increasing inequality is the inevitable consequence of capitalism's historical evolution. Piketty's contributions to the debate, and the data he amasses, are important. But we believe that r>g is not quite the right explanation, or at least not the full explanation, for the runaway growth in wealth and income inequality at the top that Piketty so thoroughly documents.

One cannot either theoretically or empirically explain the growing gap between wealth and income as the result of steady accumulation of capital goods through savings out of ordinary income. Moreover, if an increase in the amount of productive capital were responsible for the increase in wealth, we should also have seen an increase in average wages and a decline in the return to capital. Neither of these has been observed.

Much of the increase in wealth is attributable to the increase in the value of fixed assets and not the reflection of an increase in productive value. The most obvious and widespread example is the massive rise in real estate values. If the value of real estate increases thanks only to the rising price of the property it sits upon and not to physical improvements, this does not lead to a more productive economy; no workers have been hired, no wages paid, no investments made. In economic terms this gain is simply a "land rent." Some of this increase in the property value is a natural consequence of urbanization, but much is due to the *financialization* of the economy, including the increased supply of credit—credit that typically goes to those that already have wealth. Land rents are the most obvious source of rents in the economy, but economists have identified many others, including monopoly profits, drug pricing, patents, and other forms of intellectual property.

The capitalized value of rents gives rise to wealth, and so if rents increase, so will wealth. If monopoly power increases, monopoly profits will increase, and so too will the value of the monopolies—the measured wealth of the economy. But the productivity of the economy will decrease, and so too will the value of wages adjusted for inflation. Inequality will also increase.

Financialization

noun
1. The growth of the financial sector and its increased power over the real economy, including the ways the values and practices of the financial sector have shaped the rest of society.

Recent theoretical work points out that there are many other examples of such "exploitation" rents, and that changes in the rules that structure the economy can lead—and plausibly have led—to an increase in these rents and their capitalized value.[14] For instance, if the concentration of the banking system increases such that more banks are "too big to fail," meaning their individual failure could jeopardize the entire financial system, the value of banks will increase, not because the bigger banks will become more efficient, but because increased monopoly power and expectations of a government bailout at some point in the future will increase their value. In this analysis, we make a distinction between capital and wealth. Only an increase in the former necessarily encourages growth; because wealth may increase simply because there has been an increase in rents, the productive capacity of the economy may not be increasing in tandem with measured wealth. In fact, productive capacity may be falling even as wealth is increasing.

Rent-seeking

noun

1. The practice of obtaining wealth not through economically valuable activity but by extracting it from others, often through exploitation. Examples include a monopoly overcharging for its products (monopoly rents) or the drug companies getting Congress to pass a law that allows them to charge the government very high prices *and* supply fewer goods, services, and real innovation to the marketplace.

To right the economic imbalance, to reduce inequality and promote healthy growth in the real economy, we must attack the sources of those rents.

This is not about the politics of envy. The evidence of the last 35 years and the lessons of stagnation and low-wage recovery since the 2008 financial crisis show that we cannot prosper if our economic system does not create shared prosperity. This report is about how we can make our economy, our democracy, and our society work better for all Americans.

How We Got Here

In the last 30 years, sometimes under the radar, our economy, politics, and society have shifted. Where there was once a balance of powers between the private sector, labor institutions, and government, we now have forces pulling us in the direction of greater inequality. This means weak demand and reduced growth. It also means less long-term investment in education and research and development, and thus less innovation.

These forces ultimately undermine the American Dream, the belief that if you work hard and play by the rules you will succeed. Today, the life prospects of young Americans are determined largely by the income or education of their parents. We once stood out as a country that provided the greatest opportunity to succeed; now we stand out as one of the advanced economies that provide the least mobility, with a child's income more dependent on the education and income of his parents than in almost all other advanced countries.

This failure to provide a fair start and a good life for our children is of particular concern. The fact that in America today 20 percent of all children live in poverty—including 38 percent of African-American children and 30 percent of Latino children—is not only a moral issue but an economic one.[15] If we do not invest in our children, our workers, and our nation today, we will stay on track for slower growth, higher inequality, and less opportunity in the future.

Our economy was more balanced in the decades prior to 1980 and functioned remarkably well during the middle of the 20th century. Faced with the disaster of the Great Depression, Franklin D. Roosevelt put into place a series of major policy changes to counteract the overwhelming and harmful effects of unregulated banks and stock markets. The Federal Deposit Insurance Corporation ensured the safety of bank deposits; the Glass-Steagall Act separated deposit-taking banks from those engaged in investment activities, so that banks couldn't use federally insured money for high-risk speculation; the Securities and Exchange Commission enforced new market and securities laws that attempted to protect ordinary investors, preventing market manipulation and insider trading; and the National Labor Relations Act gave workers the right to bargain collectively. The combination created what John Kenneth Galbraith called "countervailing power" and enabled the country to avoid financial crisis for half a century.[16] In this golden age of capitalism the country's economy grew faster than in any other era, and while incomes grew at the top, middle, and bottom, those at the bottom saw their incomes grow faster than those at the top.

Of course, even in the golden age of capitalism, markets and the economy were not perfect. Systematic discrimination against women and people of color meant that large groups of Americans were shuttled into low-wage jobs, like domestic or janitorial work, that were not protected by unionization. African-Americans were excluded from higher education and home loan programs designed to provide opportunity to middle-income Americans.

Deprivations faced in one generation had consequences for later generations. Beginning in the 1950s, the civil rights movement fought for and made progress on desegregation, antidiscrimination, and voting access. Mobility increased during that generation, but these steps forward have not been enough. Progress has been met by obstacles, and mobility has stalled.

In the 1980s, under the influence of supply-side economic theories developed during the previous decade, and driven by conservative ideology and special interests, American policymakers began to deregulate the economy.[17] The country also lowered taxes on top earners and on the returns to capital. Then, in the 1990s, the tax on capital gains was lowered still further. Further reductions in top rates, capital gains, and dividends occurred in the beginning of this century. All of this was allegedly to encourage more work and savings. The premise was that lowering taxes would increase growth and all would benefit. Reagan argued that growth would increase so much that tax revenues would increase. The results were disappointing: the hoped-for supply-side responses were not forthcoming, tax revenues fell, and we experienced lower growth and more instability.

Supply-side economic theories

noun

1. Theories that focused on increasing the supply side of the economy—for instance making conditions more favorable for businesses and investors, or lowering taxes on workers in the hope that lower taxes would elicit a large labor supply—as opposed to the Keynesian theory that focused on demand. Supply-side theories hypothesized that improving incentives through lower tax rates and lighter regulations on business would lead to increased work, investment, and entrepreneurship, which in turn would lead to stronger growth with trickle-down benefits of higher employment, incomes, and tax revenues. The failure of these theories to live up to these predictions has left them largely discredited among economists, though they remain popular among certain conservative politicians and ideologues.

The 1990s and 2000s brought other sweeping changes. In these years, the deregulated finance sector incentivized short-termism among corporations. Much of the growth we saw in the 1990s turned out to be unstable, built on asset bubbles—first the tech bubble, then the housing bubble. The "great moderation" turned out to be a phantasm: instead of new economic insights (for instance concerning the conduct of monetary policy) leading to a better-managed economy, we had more instability, slower growth, and more inequality.

At the same time, there were changes in technology and globalization, the closer integration of the countries of the world. These advances were supposed to increase standards of living, not pose a threat to middle-class life, and they might have done that had we managed them well. But the widely accepted premise was that unfettered markets would automatically make all of us better off, and that premise turned out to be woefully wrong. While globalization and technology brought more interdependence to world markets, the lack of safeguards against a race to the bottom in labor costs meant significant job losses in the American economy and downward pressure on wages. Together with the increased financialization of the U.S. economy, these forces also contributed to the decline of vertically integrated manufacturing, which brought multiple stages of the production process under one roof.[18] The culmination of all these factors is the high-rent, high-exploitation, low-wage and low-employment American economy.

Short-termism

noun
1. The post-1980s model of corporate governance that focuses on short-term profits and returns to shareholders as opposed to the long term, including long-term investments in people and research that lead to sustainability, innovation, and growth.

Today, many place their hope in the innovative revolutions of the 1990s and 2000s: the distributed technologies enabled by the Internet, the promises of nanotechnology, and the profound possibilities of biotechnology and personalized medicine. To date, we have seen growth in some fields, the makings of strong companies, and real fortunes built on the power of the Internet. But the most important economic question is whether these technologies can help us create and distribute more growth, opportunity, and well-being to more people. Can the Internet and its yet-untapped innovative potential become the 21st century equivalent of the 20th century's manufacturing sector for Americans across income levels? Or will it add to the high-rent economy we currently face? We have seen many benefits from web technology, but we haven't yet seen it drive broadly shared prosperity. Indeed, some new technologies may tend to lead to more concentration of income, wealth, and power.

This is our challenge: For the promise of innovation to be realized, we must first solve the legacy of problems left to us by 35 years of supply-side thinking and the corresponding set of rules that has reshaped all aspects of our economy and society and led to slower growth and unprecedented inequality.

Our Story of Today's Economy

We have developed a 21st century American economy defined by low wages and high rents. Yet the rules and power dynamics embedded in today's economy are not always visible. Think of slow income growth and rising inequality as an iceberg:

- ■ The visible tip of the iceberg is everyone's daily experience of inequality: small paychecks, insufficient benefits, and insecure futures.
- ■ Just underneath the surface are the drivers of this lived experience. These are hard to see but vitally important: the laws and policies that structure the economy and create inequality. These include a tax system that raises insufficient revenue, discourages long-term investment, and rewards speculation and short-term gains; lax regulation and enforcement of rules to make corporations accountable; and the demise of rules and policies that support children and workers.
- ■ At the base are the large global forces that underlie all modern economies—drivers like technology, globalization, and demographics. These are forces to be reckoned with, but even the biggest global trends, while clearly shapers of the economy, can be shaped and pushed toward better outcomes.

The tip of the iceberg is what we see and experience. It is the most important thing to voters and politicians; it is our daily lives. But it is carried along by a mass of market-structuring forces that determine the economic and political balance of power and create winners and losers. Just as the part of the iceberg that is below the surface sinks ships, this mass of rules is what is sinking the American middle class.

Often policymakers, advocates, and the public focus only on interventions against the visible tip of the iceberg. In our political system, grand proposals to redistribute income to the most vulnerable and to curb the influence of the most powerful are reduced to modest policies like a limited earned income tax credit or transparency around executive pay. Further, some policymakers decry the value of any interventions, suggesting that the forces at the base of the iceberg are too momentous and overwhelming to control—that globalization and prejudice, climate change and technology are exogenous forces that policy cannot address. Had we curbed excesses in housing finance, this thinking goes, the financial sector would have found some other way of creating a bubble. If we curb one form of executive pay, companies will find more sophisticated routes to reward their CEOs.

This defeatist mentality concludes that the underlying forces of our economy *can't* be tackled. We disagree. There is little we can do if we don't take the laws, rules, and global forces head on. The premise of this report is that we can reshape the middle of the iceberg—the intermediating structures that determine how global forces manifest themselves.

This means that we can best improve economic security and opportunity by tackling the technocratic realms of labor law, corporate governance, financial regulation, trade agreements, codified discrimination, monetary policy, and taxation.

THE TIP OF THE ICEBERG

**DAILY
EXPERIENCE
OF INEQUALITY**
▶ Jobs that don't
pay enough to live on
▶ Rising living costs
▶ Deep anxiety

**RULES THAT STRUCTURE
OUR ECONOMY**
▶ Financial regulation and corporate
governance
▶ Tax structure
▶ International trade and finance agreements
▶ Macroeconomic policy
▶ Labor law and labor market access
▶ Structural discrimination

LARGE GLOBAL FORCES
▶ TECHNOLOGY ▶ GLOBALIZATION

The focus here on the rules of the economy and the power to set them isn't a call for the government to get out of the way. There is rarely an "out of the way" for the government. As we said earlier, markets don't exist in a vacuum; it is government that structures markets and sets the rules and regulations under which they operate. Rules and institutions are the backdrop of the economy, and the ways we set these rules, and keep them up to date and enforce them, have consequences for everyone.

The Structure of This Report

If the economy is not functioning as it should or could, then we have available to us a much broader range of policy solutions for improving growth and equality than we typically tap. The increase in inequality and the decrease in equality of opportunity have reached the point at which individual fixes that target what we can see—fixes like modest increases in the minimum wage and reforms to education and educational opportunity—will not suffice. While important, they should be seen more as short-term palliatives, providing symptomatic relief. We need a far more comprehensive approach that results in improving the market distribution of income and true opportunity across generations. An essential part of this entails dealing with the outsized growth of the financial system and its effects on private-sector behavior and decision-making throughout the economy.

In this report we cover what we consider to be the essential drivers of inequality. In the following section, "The Current Rules," we describe how public policy decisions are at the root of rising inequality and increasing insecurity. The massive overhaul of the rules of the financial sector, corporate governance, and labor law in the 1980s and 1990s has resulted in poor outcomes. Changes to the goals and conduct of monetary and fiscal policy have prioritized the wealthy. Meanwhile, efforts to make good on the American promise of inclusion have stalled, and we have failed to dismantle structures of discrimination. All of the above are the result of deliberate policy choices made with the promise that they would enhance growth, but they have ultimately resulted in an economy that is more unequal and much weaker.

Growing inequality has reached a near-crisis level. This crisis, though, is different from the financial crisis of 2008, where the alternative to action appeared to be an immediate collapse in the economy. This is a subtler crisis, but the decisions we make now will determine the nature of our economy and our society for years to come. If we take the wrong path, we are locking in greater inequality and diminished economic performance. If we take the right path, we can not only produce immediate benefits—helping preserve the middle-class life to which so many Americans aspire—but also build toward a future economy with broadly shared growth. In the final section, "Rewriting the Rules," we discuss the policy solutions that are necessary for responding to this crisis, the reforms that are needed to our underlying economic structures, and the programs that could enable more Americans to live the life they have worked so hard to achieve.

THE CURRENT RULES

Inequality has been a choice. Beginning in the 1970s, a wave of deliberate ideological, institutional, and legal changes began to reconfigure the marketplace. At the vanguard was deregulation, which, according to adherents, would loosen the constraints on the economy and free it to thrive. Next were much lower tax rates on top incomes so that money could flow to private savings and investment instead of the government. Third were cuts in spending on social welfare, to spur people to work. Get government out of the way, it was argued, and the creativity of the marketplace— and the ingenuity of the financial sector—would revitalize society.

Things didn't work out that way. First, tax revenues plummeted and deficits soared. Then we saw glimmers of the instability that would lie ahead—the financial crisis of 1989, which led to the economic recession in the early 1990s. Today, we can look back and see the toll of these "reforms": the worst economic crisis in 80 years, slower growth than in the preceding 30 years, and an unbridled increase in inequality.[1] We also now know that "deregulation" is, in fact, "reregulation"—that is, a new set of rules for governing the economy that favors a specific set of actors.

Understanding the trends of the past few decades has absorbed economists' attention in recent years. Today, labor force participation sits at a 38-year low.[2] While households had been saving, on average, less than 3 percent of income before the Great Recession, savings have increased following the recession—averaging 4.8 percent for the past year—though not enough to offset lost wealth or to make much of a dent in household indebtedness, and still not high enough to ensure sustainable growth.[3] Investment has been weak.[4] American corporations are sitting on trillions of dollars of cash, eschewing investment even though the effective corporate tax rate—the rate they actually pay on average—has fallen.[5] All of this helps explain why the promised growth did not occur: the promised supply-side effects weren't real. The economic model was wrong.

In the years since the 1970s the rules of the game changed in ways that destroyed the balance of economic power achieved in the three decades after World War II. In this section we examine the turns that have taken us down this sad road, and we consider them in the light of a few lessons learned along the way:

- Fundamental changes in the rules of the economy have led to greater inequality, not only with fewer people sharing in the economic gains, but the economy overall and even business investment growing slower as a result.

■ In the private sector, finance has gone from serving the whole economy to serving itself. Corporations have gone from serving all of their stakeholders—workers, shareholders, and management—to serving only top management under the guise of enhancing "shareholder value." And increasing the market power of a few firms in key sectors has meant that competition has less sway. The result: shortsighted behavior, underinvestment in jobs and the future, low growth, higher prices, and greater inequality.

■ Our tax system encourages speculation rather than work, distorts the economy, and serves the interests of the 1 percent.

■ In monetary and fiscal policy, focusing excessively on some threats—budget deficits and inflation—while ignoring the real threats to economic prosperity—growing inequality and underinvestment—has resulted in higher unemployment, more instability, and lower growth.

■ Changes in labor market institutions, laws, regulations, and norms have weakened worker power and made it difficult for workers to countervail the excesses of corporate and market power. The result has been a growing gap between productivity and wages, perhaps the most striking aspect of American economic life in the past third of a century.

■ These problems are exacerbated for those who suffer from discrimination and disadvantage. The market

perpetuates the transmission of advantage across generations, and discrimination has precluded large populations from developing their own human capital and
accumulating wealth.

This is a stark picture of a world gone wrong. But these have all
been choices, meaning we can choose to do things differently.
We will point toward a path forward in our final section.

More Market Power, Less Competition

- Competition is an essential feature of a successful economy,
  driving firms to be efficient and driving down prices. Competition limits the power of market actors to tip economic and
  political outcomes in their favor.
- Significant parts of the U.S. economy have strayed far from this
  competitive ideal, and market power is playing a larger role in
  areas vital to people's well-being and to the overall economy's
  performance.
- Changes in technology and globalization have played a role in
  this increase in market power. But so too have explicit policy
  choices made by government. In many cases, the government
  has chosen not to keep market power in check.
- Because such activities can decrease economic efficiency and
  stifle motivation, reining in market power will support a more
  dynamic U.S. economy, not just a more equitable one.

Textbook economics posits a world in which no one firm has
power in the marketplace. With many firms competing, no sin-

gle one has the power to raise prices and its own profits because customers can buy from any number of competitors. But in the real world market power relationships are an essential feature of our economy and are evident in numerous ways, in relationships between businesses and their customers, businesses and workers, and businesses and government.

The ability to wield power in the market is related to the degree to which markets operate in an open, transparent, competitive fashion versus the degree to which they are dominated by one or a small number of actors; how open or closed an industry is to entry by other firms; and the degree to which the same information and knowledge is shared among all participants in the market. These characteristics of a market define a spectrum of situations along which an empowered party can exercise power to varying degrees over others—even when people exchange seemingly with free will.[6] Power in the marketplace spans from the traditional "natural monopolies" we teach in Econ 101—where there is only one firm from which a typical homeowner can buy electricity, for example—to the more complicated cases where business scale and scope give a single firm, like Walmart, the power to set prices throughout the supply chain; or where a surplus of available workers in a community gives an employer the power to set wages. When we say these entities have the power to set wages or prices, we do not mean that this power is unfettered. We simply distinguish the situation where, for instance, a firm can raise its prices above its costs, increasing profits but losing relatively few customers, from the perfectly competitive market where a firm that raises prices would lose customers to competitors. For shorthand, we take "monopoly" to mean the scope of such varied power relationships in the marketplace.

Why there must be rules to ensure that markets remain free and competitive

Regulation to ensure the competitiveness of markets in the United States has a long history dating back to the Interstate Commerce Commission, created in 1887 as the first national industrial regulatory body, and the Sherman Antitrust Act of 1890, which prohibited certain mergers and anticompetitive business practices. The Sherman Act, together with the Federal Trade Commission Act and the Clayton Act, both passed in 1914, form the core of federal antitrust law. They describe unlawful business practices in fairly general terms, leaving it to the courts to decide which specific acts are illegal on a case-by-case basis.

Over time, the U.S. built a number of institutions to monitor anticompetitive practices and weigh challenges to monopoly behavior. But beginning in the 1970s, economic ideas in the field of competition emerged from free-market scholars who viewed antitrust regulation as antiquated and counterproductive in its effect on competition.[7] Many key industries, including airlines, railroads, telecommunications, natural gas, and trucking, were deregulated from the 1970s through the 1990s. Legal interpretations in regulatory rulemaking and an accumulating body of case law further limited regulatory scope and opened the domain for market power to grow unchecked.[8]

Meanwhile, the government itself can vest businesses with market power by setting the rules of the marketplace. Perhaps the most clear-cut example of the way that policies can create market power is intellectual property rights, or IPRs—the government-enforced temporary monopoly on the right to profit from an innovation. Well-being generated by innovation relies on two points: first, innovators need appropriate incentives and resources; second, innovations should be distributed widely throughout the population so that people benefit from technological advances. IPRs—patents and copyrights—in theory provide incentives for innovators by offering monopoly returns from their innovations for a limited period of time. However, in the words of economists Michele Boldrin and David K. Levine, "there is no empirical evidence that [IPRs] serve to increase innovation and productivity."[9] Other research by Petra Moser examining the long-run economic history of IPRs and innovation draws a similar conclusion.[10] Part of the reason for this is that it is not just financial incentives that matter to innovators. Among the most important discoveries are those that are part of the advancement of science, from the discovery of DNA to the mathematical insights that led to the computer (the Turing machine), rather than those made for primarily financial gain. Strong IPRs, perversely, can actually impede innovation in the economy by limiting the spillover of knowledge critical to fueling additional innovations.[11]

Though IPRs might not have much positive impact on innovation, they do have the effect of raising the prices paid to owners of intellectual properties (who often may not be the same people as those doing the innovating). Such IPRs effectively redistribute money from consumers to IPR owners—simply because government affords them greater legal protection against market competition. Artificially raising prices has the effect of shutting some people out from enjoying the benefits of innovation. This is particularly disturbing in the case of medicines, where our poorly designed IPR system, combined with a poorly designed health care system, have condemned large numbers of people to unnecessary deaths and morbidities.[12]

An innovation economy requires a *balanced* and *differentiated* intellectual property regime—combined with strong direct public support, especially for basic science and technology. Over the years, our system has lost that balance. Trade agreements, for instance, have extended the effective life of the patent by making it more difficult for generic medicines to enter the market.

Government policies also vest companies with market power through the ways in which the government buys goods and services from and sells public assets, such as mineral rights, to the private market. Procurement in the defense industry, especially under sole-source contracting (as in the case of the multi-billion-dollar Halliburton contract at the beginning of the Iraq War) is a notorious system for giveaways to government contractors.[13] Another is a provision in Medicare Part D expansion to cover part of the cost of outpatient prescription medicine, which prevented the government from using its bulk purchasing power to negotiate lower costs of medicines for senior citizens and people under 65 with certain disabilities.[14] The restriction ensured that seniors would hand more of their fixed incomes to pharmaceutical and health insurance companies and significantly raised the cost to taxpayers.

New technologies mean new sources of market power

New technologies of information and interconnectivity transform not only the way we work and live, but also the power relationships between people throughout the supply chain. Network externalities arise when an individual's benefit from using or doing something depends in part on the number of other people doing the same thing. For example, the value of joining a social networking application increases with the number of others choosing the same platform. Once these patterns are established, it becomes costly to join a different network, thus vesting the first to move into a space and attract a critical mass of joiners with substantial market powers.[15]

New economy technologies often combine network externalities with complementing economic characteristics of increasing returns to scale. This means that as production increases, the cost of producing additional units decreases, and in many such cases can reach a point of essentially zero cost for producing more. In other words, it costs essentially nothing for Google or Facebook to supply one additional advertisement to users or for Apple to supply one additional iTunes download. In such situations, competition will not be viable. Market power—and monopoly profits—may be especially large.

We also can see how companies like Uber, Airbnb, and Lending Club are innovating and disrupting the way that labor, land, and capital markets, respectively, have worked in the past. These innovations of network connectivity are in each case putting to work idle economic resources. As these and other companies engage currently monopolistic enterprises in new wave competition, and as these companies use technology to improve the efficiency with which resources get used, there is the potential for an increase in overall welfare. But in some instances, some of the advantages of these companies arises from tax and regulatory arbitrage—in circumventing regulations, for instance, which are important to promote health and safety and worker rights. And in some cases, new monopolies will be created. Thus these innovations will also raise more questions about how the gains will be distributed and how the rules that ensure fairness and conditions of work and other societal protections will be applied.

The new technologies and our out-of-balance intellectual property regime are not the only sources of market power. There is a large body of economic research on natural and artificially created barriers to entry and competition. In a fast-moving, changing economy, there are likely to be information asymmetries, and these asymmetries can lead to less competitive markets. And markets can actually act in ways that increase these information asymmetries. As we will see below, the financial market, through its lack of transparency and complexity, has excelled at this.

Globalization tilts the balance of power

Just as IPRs must balance the interests of innovators with the need for broadly dispersed innovation, so too must trade agreements balance the needs of an increasingly interconnected economy with the protection of communities, worker standards, and the environment. Our rules have not successfully balanced these forces. Our globalized world can bring new opportunities for gains for all, but also can provide opportunities for large corporations to dominate sectors of the international market, increasing market power, or to seek lowest-common-denominator labor, environmental, or tax laws.

We live in an increasingly globalized world where rules of trade and finance are important. The problem is that these rules are typically set in processes that are not transparent and democratic—with those in the industry having greater say than consumers, workers, and other citizens who are also affected. It is easy to see how such rules can increase corporate profits at the expense of workers and the environment.

Rules that make it easier for goods produced abroad to enter the U.S., that make it safer for corporations to invest abroad, that provide tax advantages for investments abroad, that do not impose environmental and labor standards on goods made abroad—all of these tilt the balance against workers. They make a threat by a firm to move its production abroad if workers don't accept lower wages or poorer working conditions more credible.

When the interests of all parties are considered, rules can redress these imbalances—for instance, with rules barring imports of products using child or prison labor, barring the use of wood from endangered forests, or barring goods produced with processes that violate other global social and environmental agreements. But we have not chosen to adopt these sorts of rules. Further, in some cases, the threat of globalization has been used as a basis for a race to the bottom. Before the 2008 crisis, the threat of globalization was used to argue for financial deregulation—if we didn't deregulate, business would move elsewhere. We now know that we lost doubly in giving in to such threats: the economic damage caused by the deregulation has been enormous, far greater than the short-term gains of the few jobs created here. And as we have seen, the changes foisted on us in this manner have undermined the long-run performance of the economy and contributed greatly to our inequality.

We could and should have used our position as the largest economy in the world to set rules that helped all parties, in the U.S. and the rest of the world.

Consequences of market power
for equity and efficiency

An increase in the market power of a firm shifts wealth from customers to the owners of those firms with market power. The decrease in the wealth of customers is not recorded in accountings of the economy's capital stock, while the increase of the value of firms is. The ranks of *Forbes* World's Billionaires are peppered with people who attained that position thanks to their monopoly power in finance, extractive industries, real estate, and privatized telecommunications.[16]

The market distortion associated with the exercise of market power diminishes social welfare. Besides creating inequalities, market rents have other distortionary effects on the economy and on the political system. First, rents directly decrease production from what it would be if the economy were organized optimally and such rents did not exist.[17] Second, rents create incentives for allocating resources to unproductive rent-seeking activities like excessive marketing and sales expenditures and lobbying; the bigger the rent, the greater the incentives for such activities.[18] For example, in 2010 the health care industry spent $102.4 million lobbying against the Affordable Care Act, while the finance and real estate industries have spent billions lobbying against passage and implementation of the Dodd-Frank financial reform law.[19] Lastly, to the degree that firms engage in lobbying or some other political activity in order to create or preserve rents, it impacts our political system—and increases the number of adverse outcomes in the economy and in other spheres of society. The original antitrust laws were motivated by the distortions to our political system as much as to our economic system.

But in order to see this impact play out, we need to look to specific markets. And one of the most dramatic examples is the growth of the financial sector, which we turn to next.

The Growth of the Financial Sector

■ The finance industry has shifted away from its essential function of allocating capital to productive uses and has moved toward predatory rent-seeking activities. In addition to catalyzing the 2008 financial crisis, these activities have slowed growth, increased the risk of future crises, and moved income from the bottom and middle to the top, increasing inequality.

■ Widespread deregulation and malign regulatory neglect, beginning in the 1970s and continuing through the early 2000s, enabled reckless growth and malfeasance in America's financial sector.

■ Much of the increased incomes of the top 1 percent arise from the enormous, unwarranted profits and bonuses collected in the financial sector and derived, in no small part, from wasteful and exploitative activities.

As the rules of the U.S. financial system changed over the past generation, the financial sector grew to play a larger, more dominant role in the U.S. economy. The rise of finance twisted incentives within both finance and the nonfinancial economy and pulled more of the economy's rewards from the real economy into finance and from working families up to the executive suites. Specifically, financial profits and financial salaries have increasingly come at the expense of the income and savings of everyone else. The inequities have been exacerbated by open and hidden subsidies—not just massive bailouts (of which the 2008 bailout was only the biggest and most recent) but by provisions hidden in the tax system and bankruptcy code that enrich those in the financial sector at the expense of the public.

Finance's failure to self-regulate

A growing economy requires a well-functioning financial system. The financial sector is essential to running the payment systems, ensuring a flow of funds from savers to investors, including small and medium-sized enterprises, and creating information and opportunities for investment. The financial sector is also necessary for diversifying investments, managing risk, and providing liquidity and other resources necessary for growth.

However, finance needs rules, and the 2008 financial crisis revealed once again that financial markets cannot regulate themselves. Certain features of financial markets make them more subject to failure than most other kinds of markets. First, activities people undertake in the financial industry create large externalities, both positive and negative. Financial instability, in particular contagious runs and self-fulfilling panics, can impose massive costs on the economy.[20] Economists at the Dallas Federal Reserve estimate that the costs of the 2008 financial crisis amounted to 40–90 percent of one year's GDP, as much as $16 trillion in today's terms.[21] Since the beginning of financial deregulation in the United States and around the world, financial crises have been increasing in frequency and severity.[22]

Second, financial markets are plagued with asymmetries of information—situations where one party knows more than the other. The existence of such asymmetries is inevitable, of course, but their magnitude is not, nor is the right to exploit others by taking advantage of these asymmetries. Third, financial markets are lacking in industry competition. In particular, since the 1970s, the concentration, scale, and scope of the largest banks have grown significantly and rapidly, with the share of industry assets held by the top five banks growing from 17 percent to 52 percent.[23]

Starting in the late 1970s, the financial industry lobbied for and policymakers largely delivered a rollback of regulation with the promise that the financial sector would self-regulate.[24] Changes to the rules of finance, many of which were in place since financial collapse sparked the Great Depression, removed the separation of commercial and investment banking, ceilings on deposit rates, and prohibitions on usury—the charging of loan-shark level interest rates. The changes didn't update the rules for new instruments like derivatives, but they let the financial markets write their own rules as they expanded into securities that packaged mortgages. Enforcement became an issue, with federal regulators appointed who didn't believe in regulation. They overruled state-level regulations and enforced less than vigorously the limited regulations that remained.[25]

The growth of finance and inequality

Changes to these rules are one of the major drivers of inequality. First, finance has become huge and profitable relative to the rest of the economy. Financial services comprised 7.6 percent of GDP before the crisis, then fell back slightly to 6.6 percent in 2012 before returning to 7.3 percent in 2014. By way of comparison, in the 1950s, when the U.S. economy was growing rapidly, more rapidly than in recent years, financial services constituted 2.8 percent of GDP. Between 1950 and 1980 the financial sector generated between 10 and 20 percent of total corporate profits; financial sector profits rose to 26 percent of total by the end of the 1980s, held this level on average during the 1990s expansion, and then rose to a peak of 46 percent in 2001 and averaged 32 percent in the 2000s expansion before the Great Recession.[26]

This is mirrored in the skyrocketing salaries in the financial sector, which have been a major driver of the top 1 percent. Wages in the financial sector rose more than in similar fields, with the increase closely following the trend of deregulation.[27] Between 1979 and 2005, finance professionals increased their presence among the top 1 percent by 80 percent (from 7.7 to 13.9 percent).[28] They have also increased their presence amongst the top 0.1 percent, from 11 percent in 1979 to 18 percent by

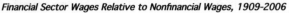

COMPENSATION IN FINANCE PULLED AWAY FROM THE REST AFTER 1980

Financial Sector Wages Relative to Nonfinancial Wages, 1909-2006

FIGURE 1

Source: Philippon, Thomas and Ariell Reshef. 2012. "Wages and Human Capital in the U.S. Financial Industry 1909-2006." Quarterly Journal of Economics.

2005, and have accounted for 70 percent of the growth in the 0.1 percent's share of national income.[29] No other sector shows this kind of growth during this period. Figure 1 reproduces data from economists Thomas Phillipon and Ariell Reshef showing wages in the financial sector relative to those in the rest of the nonfinancial, nonfarm economy. Financial sector wages follow a similar U-shaped pattern as overall inequality, having fallen from the Great Depression until 1980 and rising since 1980; those wages rise statistically with deregulation.[30] While in 1980 wages in the financial sector were basically on par with wages in the rest of the economy, by 2006 the average wage in finance was 72 percent higher than the average nonfinancial wage. These wages can't be explained solely by skills; research argues that rents account for 30–50 percent of these higher wages, especially since the late 1990s.[31]

Weaker financial rules create a weaker economy

The last 35 years of deregulation have had profound consequences for average Americans and the country's overall economic performance. Rent-seeking fees on each of the areas in which banks operate, from running the payments mechanism to managing investment activity have bloated the financial sector, while a dangerous form of banking and lending ultimately drove the economy to collapse.

Financial market regulation aims to minimize discrimination and exploitation, but in the deregulated system we've seen significant evidence of systemic predatory lending, fraud, and discrimination, aimed at taking advantage of lower-income borrowers.[32] Borrowers with low financial literacy are more likely to have costly mortgages and not to understand or remember the terms of their mortgage contracts.[33]

In addition, the opaqueness and complexity of the financial sector and the weak enforcement of the rules that remained encouraged widespread fraud and manipulation. A recent target of market manipulation has been the LIBOR rate (the London Interbank Offered Rate, meant to be an objective measure of the costs of funds to banks), which determines the interest rate millions of homeowners pay for their mortgages and which underlies more than $300 trillion worth of securities.[34] Foreign exchange markets have also been manipulated.[35] Lack of competition in many parts of the financial system—including in the credit and debit card systems, asset management, and derivatives markets—has meant higher profits for banks and higher costs for consumers and ordinary citizens.

Indeed, a key source of growth in the profits of the financial sector comes from asset management activities, which include both the management of 401(k)s and mutual funds, as well as alternative investment vehicles (investments beyond the conventional stocks, bonds, and mutual funds) like private equity and hedge funds. The growth in asset management income accounts for roughly 35 percent of the growth of the financial sector as a percent of GDP, driven by the opaque fee structures, especially when it comes to alternative investment vehicles.[36] But in spite of their high fees, there is little evidence of any advantages, for instance in better long-run performance, when it comes to higher management fees.[37] Other key sources of financial profits have come from their privileged position in running the economy's payments system: ATM and sundry other fees levied on normal saving and checking accounts.

Another core growth business for finance has been shadow banking, or the moving of traditional commercial banking functions to the financial markets. Shadow banking shares many of the same features of traditional banking—connecting savers with borrowers. However, the long chains in the provision of credit are complex and nontransparent, creating leverage and additional sources of financial risk and more vulnerability to fraud and other misbehavior. This is especially true for mortgages, where originators, investment banks, the credit-rating agencies, and mortgage insurers were all on the scene. In more than one case, there was fraud to an unconscionable degree. It should have been apparent that shadow banking was vulnerable to runs—where everyone pulls their money out at the same time—the moment the value of the collateral was questioned, as was the case when the 2008 failure of Lehman Brothers caused panic and contagion across the economy.[38]

Shadow banks

noun
1. The array of institutions that provide financial services but operate outside of the laws and regulations applied to traditional banks that are designed to ensure oversight and accountability of traditional lending banks.

When this system crashed, its complicated structure led to multiple conflicts of interest. Many of the debt servicers (those responsible for collecting monthly payments, who were also tasked to handle bad loans) actually profited from making those mortgages worse from the perspective of both lenders and homeowners. Studies have also shown that troubled mortgages were significantly less likely to receive a modification, enabling distressed homeowners to stay in their homes, if they were made through this shadow banking system rather than through traditional banks.[39]

A growing and healthy financial system is essential to

growth. But what if financial markets become too large? It would be one thing if the increased incomes of the financial sector had resulted in the economy growing faster or in a more stable way. In fact, just the opposite has occurred. Figure 2 shows estimates, again by economist Thomas Philippon, of the average cost of the U.S. financial sector of supplying one dollar of financial intermediation—connecting savers with borrowers—from 1884 to 2011. Incredibly, the data show that the U.S. financial sector is less efficient now at supplying credit to the economy. The average cost was 2.4 cents on the dollar in 2011, compared to 1.6 cents at the end of World War II.[40] This is in spite of the

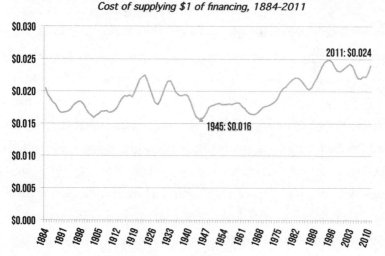

U.S. FINANCIAL INDUSTRY EVEN LESS EFFICIENT AFTER MORE THAN A CENTURY

Cost of supplying $1 of financing, 1884-2011

FIGURE 2

Source: Philippon, Thomas. 2014. "Has the US Finance Industry Become Less Efficient?" American Economic Review.

technological advances that should have significantly lowered the costs of transactions.

It is remarkable that for all the growth in income, profits, and size of the financial sector, we cannot see any improvement in the performance of the economy. The sector may have demonstrated innovation, but the technological advances chased a greater ability to exploit others rather than improving economic performance. And many are concerned that as the financial sector has grown too large, and paid excessive compensation to its top employees, it has drawn talented people and energy away from more productive enterprises.[41]

The Dodd-Frank Act, passed by Congress in 2010, began the process of restructuring the financial sector. But even as passed, it was a compromise, and its rule-writing and enforcement hasn't done enough to tackle the shadow banking system, the complexity of the financial system, and the problem of too-big-to-fail banks. But the remarkable aspect of this reform was that it was all about preventing the financial sector from doing harm to the rest of the economy, taking advantage of the unwary, and engaging in reckless risk taking. It was *not* directed at ensuring that the financial sector actually does what it is supposed to do: make money available for productive uses.[42] This still remains an essential task, one that can't be examined without understanding the massive changes in corporate governance taking place at this time as well.

The "Shareholder Revolution," the Rise of CEO Pay, and the Squeezing of Workers

- Corporations are a social construct, providing limited liability, an important component of modern capitalism. But they often fail to serve the public interest, and instead enrich those who are entrusted with their care while neglecting the corporation's own long-term interests, let alone those of their workers and the communities in which they operate.
- The shareholder revolution transformed the incentives faced by CEOs, prodding them to generate ever-higher share prices in the short run by tying executive compensation to those share prices.
- The emphasis on short-term stock prices has not only reduced investment that leads to healthy innovation and long-term prosperity, but also has encouraged managers to treat employees as short-term liabilities rather than as long-term assets. In the financial sector, in particular, the compensation schemes led not only to short-term behavior but also excessive risk-taking. At the same time, executive compensation has increased to levels that cannot be justified by their productivity; these increases have come at the expense of workers, investment, and shareholders, and have contributed to the country's growing inequality.
- The job tenure of the average CEO also shortened, further exacerbating the disparity between the short-term interests of management and those of long-term stakeholders.
- A number of changes to tax, pension, corporate governance, and securities law have encouraged these destructive short-term corporate behaviors.

The idea that corporations exist solely to maximize *current* shareholder value and that all other goals are secondary reversed decades of management theory that prioritized firm longevity and saw corporations as more broadly advancing societal interests. This means that short-term strategies to raise profits would take precedence over more farsighted ones such as long term investments, including in innovation, serving consumers, and investing in employees—all which increase long-term corporate values. This "shareholder revolution" has meant significant changes for the economy. The new emphasis on maximizing shareholder value was a key step toward short-termism on Wall Street and in corporate boardrooms, and it has had profound effects for corporate performance and economic productivity.

Even John Maynard Keynes, who worried about the effects of short-term speculation on the economy 80 years ago, would probably be surprised at the extent of short-termism today. While the average stock was held for around seven years in 1940 and two years in 1987, by 2007 the average share was traded every seven months.[43] With the average shareholder interested only in short-term performance, shareholder value maximization translates into short-termism: focusing on quarterly returns, and even on accounting tricks to massage quarterly earnings. Where the goal of finance should be to provide needed cash to the productive economy, the shareholder revolution transformed corporations into sources of cash for financiers. This trend toward short-termism is seen in rising executive pay, increasing payouts to stockholders, frequent corporate restructurings, massive mergers, and reduced capital investment. These trends increase economic inequity and threaten long-term economic performance.

The rules give rise to shareholder primacy

The rise of shareholder primacy has been aided and abetted by the practices of financial markets and the theories of conservative economists. But above all it was a change in the rules of the market—specifically in securities law and federal income tax law—that combined to give more power to institutional investors and tie executive pay to short-term returns.[44] The first wave of this revolution was conducted through leveraged buyouts, in which investors aimed to take over large companies, "unlock" hidden value (usually by downsizing), and sell quickly. The ability to conduct leveraged buyouts this way was the result of changes in U.S. regulations—including exemptions for leveraged buyout funds from the Investment Company Act—and legal interpretations. In the 1982 case *Edgar v. MITE*, the Supreme Court struck down Illinois's antitakeover law and thereby overturned similar laws in other states.[45] This made takeovers easier—including those wishing to take over the firm to get access to its cash and to "restructure" it in ways that benefited the takeover artists at the expense of everyone else. The Reagan administration also relaxed antitrust regulations, facilitating the ability of one firm to take over its rivals and reducing competition in the market.[46]

The result of these and other legal and regulatory changes was a rash of takeovers. In the 1980s, half of all U.S. corporations were the objects of takeover bids. In many years, over 10 percent of total stock market capitalization was purchased in acquisitions.[47] After the 1980s, institutional investors started taking larger stakes in corporations. If all of this had led to more efficient and innovative corporations, that would have been one thing. But in fact, the new "activist" investors pushed for seats on boards and pressured management into policies that were viewed as more "shareholder-friendly"—meaning friendlier to the short-term investor—including increasing dividends and buyouts. The new generation of CEOs increasingly aligned its management style with short-term investor interests.

These changes too were aided by changes in the rules. In the 1980s, the Securities and Exchange Commission weakened insider trading rules that effectively treated company stock buybacks as per se insider trading. In the early 1990s, the SEC eliminated complicated disclosure requirements for communications between shareholders.[48] In 1993, Congress changed the tax code, supposedly to incentivize companies to tie executive pay to performance, tilting compensation toward stock options; but in fact, there was little link between the firm's long-term performance and compensation through stock options—and indeed, little link between how managers performed and the stock's performance.

There were other changes at play that contributed to the

momentum toward shorter holding periods in the capital markets—for instance, the elimination of fixed brokerage commis-
sions in the 1970s reduced the costs of buying and selling.

Rule changes make executive pay soar

While these changes have not led to a better-performing economy, they have had the effect that many of the executive advocates of this "revolution" had hoped: incomes at the top have
increased enormously. Executives of nonfinancial companies
make up over 30 percent of the top 1 percent, and their incomes
have grown significantly since the 1970s.[49] While average CEO
pay remained relatively constant at around $1 million adjust-
ing for inflation from the mid-1930s to the mid-1970s, in 2012
average compensation for the 500 highest-paid CEOs was $30.3
million, of which only 6.3 percent was salaries and bonuses.[50]
The rest is largely driven by gains from stocks and stock options
given to executives as a substitute for salary. The value of these,
in turn, is driven by stock prices. CEO pay has skyrocketed far
above the rate of employee pay. In 1965, the ratio of the average
annual income of CEOs to workers was 20-to-1. By 2013, it was
295-to-1.[51]

CEO pay packages lead to weaker investment

For all these massive changes, the broader effects of this shareholder revolution were markedly different from those that had

been anticipated. First, shareholder value maximization often turned into CEO income maximization. In practice, the interests of senior management took precedence over the interests of shareholders and other stakeholders as well. Stock options did not align the interests of management with those of the firm, as was seen in the conflict over disclosure of executive pay, including stock options, that arose in the 1990s.[52] Indeed, these pay packages have given CEOs an incentive to manipulate stock prices by using company money to buy back shares in order to drive the price higher.[53] They induced managers to engage in "creative accounting" to increase short-term profits—even if in doing so, long-term returns were lowered. Thus, managerial attention is shifted away from a focus on actual performance. This undermines the efficiency of the economy.[54]

A closer look at CEO compensation shows that there is little relationship between pay and performance. Compensation goes up when firm performance goes up, but it also goes up when performance goes down. CEOs are often compensated simply for luck, such as when oil company executives get paid more when global oil prices increase. The effect is stronger in more weakly governed firms.[55] Current economic theories seeking to justify high CEO pay, such as those that link CEO pay to an increase in firm size, cannot explain trends in CEO compensation between the 1940s and 1970s. Somewhere in the 1980s, CEO pay changed.[56] Finally, increasing shareholder value in the short run is different from serving the interests of shareholders in the long run. Empirical studies have shown that stock market prices have difficulty incorporating information more than five years out.[57] Thus rewarding managers on the basis of today's stock gives them little incentive to care about the long term.

Beyond questionable behavior from CEOs, the second worrying consequence of the shareholder revolution is a bias against real investments. Research has found that short-term pressures can distort the individual investment decisions managers make. New proprietary data show that public firms invest substantially less and are less responsive to changes in investment opportunities compared to similar private firms. This result is amplified for firms with stock prices most sensitive to earnings news. This tells us that rather than encouraging CEOs to invest, pay incentives are now tipped toward underinvestment.[58]

Research has shown a dramatic shift in the relationship between borrowing and investment, as shown in Figure 3. Before the 1980s, a firm that borrowed a dollar would, on average, invest 40 cents more. Since the 1980s this relationship has collapsed. Instead, today the strong relationship is between shareholder payouts and borrowing, with shareholder payouts nearly doubling since the 1980s. Corporate profits are at record highs, with no increase in investment. Where before finance was a mechanism for getting money into firms, now it functions to get money out of them.[59]

This problem is not going away. Even after the financial crisis, when firms were facing problems getting access to credit, firms continued buying back their own stock and paying divi-

BUSINESSES USED TO BORROW TO MAKE INVESTMENTS. NOW?
Correlation coefficient between firm borrowing and firm investment

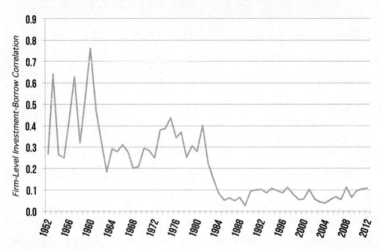

FIGURE 3

Source: Mason, J. W. 2015. "Disgorge the Cash: The Disconnect Between Corporate Borrowing and Investment." The Roosevelt Institute.

dends at a very high level.[60] Executives at nonfinancial corporations in the U.S. distributed 70 percent of pre-tax corporate profits paying shareholders in the form of stock buybacks and dividends in 2014; in the four quarters before the September 2008 financial collapse, corporations spent on average 107 percent of profits buying their own shares and paying dividends. In the postwar period before the shareholder revolution, nonfinancial corporations distributed an average 18 percent of profits to shareholders.[61] As Laurence D. Fink, the CEO of the large asset management firm BlackRock, recently wrote, "the effects of the short-termism phenomenon are troubling both to those seeking to save for long-term goals such as retirement and for our broader economy," because they are at the expense of "innovation, skilled work forces, or essential capital expenditures necessary to sustain long-term growth."[62]

Lower Taxes for the Wealthy

■ The reduced progressivity of the U.S. tax code has contributed to increased income and wealth inequality at the top.
■ Current incentives allow and encourage rent-seeking, channeling government revenue away from productive resources.
■ There is no evidence that a lower tax rate for the wealthy has encouraged investment or growth.

Myriad changes in the tax and transfer system over the past 35 years have reduced the progressivity of the tax code to the point where, in some respects, the overall system is now regressive. Shrinking capital gains and corporate rates, growth in the payroll tax, and growing tax expenditures have decreased the progressivity of effective rates and shrunk the tax base.[63] This has blunted the ability of taxes and transfers to push against increasing inequality.[64] Additionally, these changes have distorted incentives by increasing the returns to rent seeking, thus compounding inequalities built into the tax code.[65] To make matters worse, there is no evidence that lower tax rates have led to increased growth.

A tax revolution for those at the top

The rules of tax policy underwent a revolution over the past 40 years, one designed to radically lower the top marginal tax rates and decrease the progressivity of the tax code. The result was that those at the top paid less, leaving the rest to pay more tax or receive lower levels of public service. During the 1980s, for example, the top marginal tax rate was reduced from 70 percent to 28 percent, and has stayed below 40 percent ever since.[66]

In addition to low marginal income tax rates, two provisions of capital gains taxation reduce the effective capital gains tax rate. First, capital gains are not taxed until they are realized, meaning that a 20-year investment—say buying and holding a stock—generates no tax liability until the owner sells his shares. Second, a rule for readjusting the value of an inherited asset, the step-up in basis at death, largely eliminates capital gains for many of the very wealthiest families, effectively forever. Step-up in basis allows someone who inherits an asset only to pay taxation on the capital gains that have occurred since the asset passed on to him or her; as those assets get passed down through the generations, the capital gains earned during the lifetime of those making bequests never get taxed, lowering federal revenue by an estimated $644 billion between 2013 and 2023.[67] The benefits of this provision accrue almost entirely to the very top: In 2013, 65 percent of all inherited capital gains tax forgone accrued to the top 20 percent; the top 1 percent alone accounted for 21 percent. Changes in the threshold below which no inheritance tax is levied mean that an astonishingly low number of people in America are wealthy enough to pay estate taxes—in 2011, just 0.1 percent of inheritors paid any estate tax—but popular pressure is still strong to eliminate them.[68]

Beyond capital gains, tax expenditures—money the government spends to incentivize certain behaviors by offering tax deductions—and transfers have shifted from favoring low-income households to favoring the wealthy, decreasing overall progressivity. The expansion of expenditures like 401(k) retirement plans and mortgage interest deductibility has led to a decrease in effective rates at the top as more and more wealthy families take advantage of various tax breaks.[69] According to an analysis by the Congressional Budget Office, more than half of the $900 billion paid in individual income tax expenditures and 80 percent of the tax deductions in 2013 accrued to households in the top 20 percent, with 17 percent accruing to the top 1 percent, while those in the middle income quintile received just 13 percent and those in the lowest 20 percent of income received just 8 percent.[70] At the same time, transfer payments, the direct and in-kind payments that the government makes to individuals, receded.[71] According to the CBO, "In 1979, households in the bottom quintile received more than 50 percent of transfer payments. In 2007, similar households received about 35 percent of transfers."[72]

Unbalanced tax cuts increase inequality

The reduction in high-end taxes has had two effects on inequality. The first has been to reduce the ability of taxes and transfers to lessen inequality. But the second, more surprising effect is that it has massively increased pre-tax income for those at the top, far beyond what could be understood from people simply working harder. It is this new incentive to rent-seek that is a more worrying effect of the changing of the tax rules.

The combined impact of rate cuts, shifting income distribution, and growing expenditures has been to increase after-tax-and-transfer inequality both in nominal terms and relative to pre-tax-and-transfer inequality. A 2011 study by the Congressional Budget Office found that "the equalizing effect of transfers and taxes on household income was smaller in 2007 than it had been in 1979." Over this time, changes to the U.S. tax structure reduced "the extent to which taxes lessened the dispersion of household income."[73]

Capital gains income accrues disproportionately to the richest Americans; therefore, a low capital gains rate has direct implications for inequality.[74] Capital income makes up about 40 percent of annual gross income for Americans earning over $1 million a year, compared to less than 4 percent for people earning below $200,000.[75] The impact on distribution is clear: between 1996 and 2006, changes in capital gains and dividend income were the largest contributor to the increase in overall after-tax-and-transfer income inequality.[76]

Because capital gains income is concentrated at the top, and because a low capital tax has not delivered trickle-down economic performance, the benefit of the low capital gains rate is concentrated at the top. According to the CBO, 68 percent of the $161 billion annual capital gains tax expenditure goes to the top 1 percent, while only 7 percent goes to the bottom four-fifths of Americans.[77] This concentration among the wealthy gets even starker the higher up the income distribution you go. In 2009, the top 400 taxpayers—the wealthiest 0.003 percent—claimed a full 12 percent of the benefits of reduced capital gains tax rates.[78]

What is more interesting is the effect of lowering top tax rates on the highest earners. As shown in Figure 4, economists

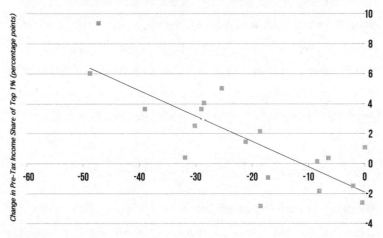

ACROSS THE WORLD, CUTTING TOP MARGINAL TAX RATES INCREASED INEQUALITY
Change in Top Marginal Pre-Tax Rate (Percentage Points)

FIGURE 4

Source: Piketty, Thomas, Emmanuel Saez and Stefanie Stantcheva. 2014. "Optimal Taxation of Top Labor Incomes: A Tale of Three Elasticities." American Economic Journal: Economic Policy, *6(1): 230-71.*

Thomas Piketty, Emmanuel Saez, and Stefanie Stantcheva find that countries that cut their highest marginal tax rates the most had the largest increases in pre-tax inequality, and these tax cuts played no role in boosting growth in per capita income. These increases are impossible to explain with a standard supply-side model, especially as the authors find no relationship between top rates and growth.[79]

The authors find that the tax rule influences top income earners to engage in more rent-seeking and attempt to get more of the economic pie for themselves rather than expanding the size of the economic pie.[80] At higher marginal tax rates, CEOs and other executives in the top 1 percent have less of an incentive to either bargain aggressively for themselves or seek opportunities for extracting rents. Similarly, other stakeholders in the firm, including shareholders and board members, also will be reluctant to pay out superstar salaries if a large portion of that income is going to the government through taxes. This is also reflected in the way pre-tax income inequality for working-age people in the United States exceeds that of other advanced economies.[81]

Lower rates have done nothing for growth

According to advocates of cuts to top marginal tax rates, the reduction was supposed to encourage more work among top earners and increase the size of the pie. But there is no evidence that this has happened.

As a Congressional Research Service report found, there

exists "no conclusive evidence . . . to substantiate a clear relationship between the 65-year reduction in the top statutory tax rates and economic growth." Cutting top tax rates did, however, "appear to be associated with the increasing concentration of income at the top of the income distribution."[82] This accords precisely with the results shown in Figure 4. If high marginal tax rates act as a deterrent to rent-seeking, strongly progressive taxation can help enhance performance of the overall economy by deterring socially unproductive activities and directing more resources into real investment.[83]

Rather than showing economic benefits from lower tax rates at the top, the evidence shows rather that progressivity can have a net economic benefit. Economist Jonathan Ostry and co-authors at the International Monetary Fund tested how the degree of progressivity of tax and transfers affects long-run economic growth when accounting for a range of other explanatory factors commonly seen as associated with economic growth.[84] Their results find that, across countries, redistribution, outside of some extremes, has no relationship with economic growth. If anything, a number of redistributive policies can lower net inequality and drive more durable growth.

Similarly, evidence from the 2003 dividend tax cut shows that this supply-side tax cuts did not lead to rising wages or investment. Indeed, there were good reasons to suspect that companies would take advantage of the low taxes to pay out large dividends, impairing their ability to invest.[85] Not surprisingly, comparing corporations that benefitted from this cut with those that did not reveals that the dividend tax cut did not result in any real investment or wage growth. The only effect was to increase dividend payments, causing more money to leave the firm rather than being invested.[86]

Recent research has shown that eliminating preferential taxes on capital income is welfare-enhancing.[87] Low tax rates on the return to capital create an enormous incentive for income shifting, through which corporations and individuals redefine labor income as capital income and drive down their effective rates. This leads to lost revenue and, by inordinately benefiting wealthier taxpayers who have more tax avoidance savvy and resources, a significant decrease in the progressivity of the tax structure.[88]

What the tax rate should be depends, of course, on how sensitive labor supply and savings are to tax rates. But using the best available evidence, it appears that there is significant room to increase tax rates above current levels.[89]

The End of Full-Employment Monetary Policy

- The Federal Reserve's focus on controlling inflation rather than achieving full employment and managing systemic financial risk has raised unemployment and lowered wages over the past 35 years.
- The Fed's failure to ensure competition in banking and financial markets has meant that the benefits of lower interest rates have often accrued more to the banks than to borrowers and that certain market segments have lacked access to credit.

> ■ Low- and middle-income households bear a disproportionate amount of the burden of prolonged recessions, financial crises, and an underperforming economy. Unemployment affects those in the bottom half of the income distribution more than those in the top half, and its effects compound over the course of people's lifetimes.

The Federal Reserve's monetary policy usually falls beyond the scope of traditional policy debates, especially those focusing on inequality. But monetary policy set by the nation's "independent" central bank can have profound distributional consequences, contributing substantially to the rise of income and wealth of those at the top and the increasing financial stress and stagnant wages faced by most working families.

The Fed's inflation preoccupation

In 1978, the Full Employment and Balanced Growth Act, also known as the Humphrey-Hawkins Act, established price stability and full employment as the dual objectives of national economic policy. Both of these objectives are part of the Federal Reserve's "dual mandate," the goals that Congress sets in delegating the conduct of monetary policy authority to the Fed.[90]

At the time, the country faced high inflation. Under Federal Reserve Chairman Paul Volcker, inflation fell from double digits in 1979 to just 4 percent in 1984, and the ability of monetary policy to control inflation was widely heralded.[91] To be sure, there were significant costs: the U.S. experienced what was then its deepest recession since the Great Depression in spite of a highly simulative tax cut.[92] Nonetheless, many countries, beginning with New Zealand in 1990, made price stability—so-called "inflation-targeting"—the sole or primary goal of monetary policy.[93] The Federal Reserve, maintaining its dual mandate, did not formally adopt this framework, but it did adopt an apparent preference for targeting low, stable inflation over maximum employment.[94] Thus, although the Fed maintains discretion as it considers tradeoffs between price stability and employment, in practice it tends to give considerable priority to pursuing low inflation—or at least that was the case until very recently.

Some simplistic models of the economy that became fashionable among central banks reinforced these views. These theories argue that unemployment can be decreased by monetary policy only to a point; if unemployment is pushed below its natural level, inflation will accelerate, and eventually the government will have to raise interest rates a great deal, resulting in higher unemployment.[95] These theoretical ideas have been largely discredited. In contrast, the idea of hysteresis posits that there are serious long-term effects of unemployment because those who become unemployed might end up outside the labor market and find it more difficult to find jobs later.[96] Deflationary pressures can raise the real value of debt, which can create self-fulfilling prophecies of low demand.[97] Low inflation, rather than something to be valued, can limit the options central bankers have in a crisis.

Central banks can't ignore inflation, but neither should they make it their main preoccupation, at least so long as it remains moderate. As the Great Recession made clear, the focus on inflation did not ensure high growth or economic stability. The choice to focus on inflation or full employment is not technocratic, but rather a choice to prioritize one set of economic outcomes and interest groups over another. In the early stages of business cycle recoveries, fearful of impending inflation, monetary policymakers have tightened money prematurely, precluding a return to full employment and ensuring that workers can't make up for the losses they suffered in the downturn. The three most recent recessions have been followed by recoveries in which labor markets were too slack to allow workers to share in the benefits of economic growth, partly because policymakers were too worried about inflation and believed it would set in at relatively low levels of unemployment.[98]

Consequences of deprioritizing the full employment mandate

While economists debate the effects of inflation on inequality, the effects of employment are clear.* Sustained periods of full employment are essential to a well-functioning economy and

---

* Unanticipated inflation hurts bondholders—who are predominately wealthy. However, wages of workers often lag behind increases in prices, so they too suffer from inflation. Econometric studies looking across countries at the effects of inflation (which typically show an association between inflation and inequality) can, however, be misleading. The major episodes of inflation were associated with increases in oil prices, and with governments that seemed unable to respond effectively.

prosperity for low- and middle-income families, while high unemployment, because of its long-term consequences, has serious repercussions for the economy as a whole.

Estimates show that for every additional percentage point of unemployment, income declines by 2.2 percent for families at the 20th percentile of the distribution, by 1.4 percent for median-income families, and by just 0.7 percent for families at the 95th percentile; these different levels of exposure to unemployment risk are a product of increasing inequality.[99] Furthermore, unemployment rates for low-skilled and minority workers rise most strongly in response to contractionary monetary policy.[100] Compared to higher-income workers, whose working hours are relatively stable, lower-income workers see larger cuts in hours worked when the unemployment rate is high.[101]

Full employment is fundamental for well-distributed economic prosperity. When the economy is at full employment and labor markets are tight, workers have greater bargaining power, since employers are forced to raise compensation to attract and retain employees. As a result, and as experience shows, the only times we see broadly shared benefits of economic growth are when the economy nears full employment. When labor markets are slack, especially in an era of reduced private-sector collective bargaining, worker bargaining power is low, and low and middle wages stagnate. Economist Alan Blinder has found that inequality rarely declines when unemployment is above 6 percent.[102]

Moreover, episodes of below-full employment do lasting damage to productivity, equity, and opportunity. New workers, such as recent graduates, who enter the labor market during a recession face weak earnings potential even a decade later.[103] Wage erosion in a recession will not necessarily be offset by wage growth in an expansion. An unemployed worker will find it harder to subsequently find employment and may even drop out of the labor force. In bad times, lower-income households may underinvest in education and human capital formation.

The Fed's excessive focus on inflation detracts from its responsibility for maintaining economic stability. The recent financial crisis and Great Recession demonstrate how middle-class households bear a disproportionate burden from financial crashes and a volatile and underperforming economy.

Even now, many look to prioritize concerns about inflation over those of full employment. The good news is that there is now a growing recognition that the unemployment rate is not the only measure of labor market slack. In the past five years, the labor market has been weaker than the unemployment rate would appear to indicate because discouraged job-seekers have dropped out of the labor force and many people are working part-time but would prefer to work full-time. Alternative indicators of underemployment help explain rising inequality and wage stagnation.[104]

This monetary aspect of economic policy, one that has been largely viewed as a technocratic debate not relevant to the average American, has large and persistent effects on inequality. Historically, we have recognized this. The election of 1896 was contested on the issue of monetary policy—whether to move to a bimetallic standard (gold and silver). The debate then was about inflation versus growth, and about inequality—the conflict between low- and middle-income Americans, then overwhelmingly farmers, and the financial sector. Somehow, in the 120 years that have elapsed since, we have made very little progress.[105] Monetary policy hewing to a rule that prioritizes low inflation at the expense of low unemployment has weakened the position of people who work for their living and strengthened those whose income relies on the return to capital.

The Stifling of Worker Voice

- A sustained political attack, dating back to the late 1970s, has weakened unions and workers' rights, while labor policies have not kept up with changes in the modern workplace.
- Decreased bargaining power has given corporations the upper hand in the labor market, weakening wages, benefits, and working conditions, and leaving managers and owners with a larger share of profits.
- Unions provide a countervailing force to corporate interests; weak unions upset the country's political balance of power as well as the economic balance of power, allowing corporate interests to act unchecked.

The right to freely associate and bargain collectively is universally recognized as a basic human right, but in the United States the ability of workers to organize has been greatly diminished by a decades-long campaign to erect barriers to unionization, place restrictions on union activity, and weaken labor laws across the board.[106] It is not just the migration of manufacturing from the more unionized North, first to the American South and then offshore, that led to deunionization. Organizing efforts have been stymied in nonmanufacturing industries, too, as well as in resurgent manufacturing bases.[107] Consequently, union participation in the United States fell from over 30 percent in 1960 to 20 percent in 1984 and 11.1 percent in 2014.[108]

The decoupling of labor productivity and hourly compensation is perhaps the clearest sign that something has gone wrong. Over the 40 years between 1973 and 2013, productivity grew 161 percent while compensation rose only 19 percent.[109] The dissolving strength, number, and effectiveness of unions has perpetuated inequality as a diminished role for unions leads to a system in which corporate interests drown out the voice of labor, forcing workers to accept weak wage growth and an eroding standard of living.

Increased corporate influence at the cost of workers' rights

The overall decline of collective bargaining was not inevitable. Despite facing similar evolutions in technology and globalization, other developed countries have recorded far less union decline. In Canada, for example, unionization rates are not much changed from their 1960s level.[110] Among all OECD countries, an average of 54 percent of the workforce is covered by union collective bargaining agreements, 4.5 times more than in the U.S.[111]

While the decline of the U.S. manufacturing industry has contributed to the decline of collective bargaining, a host of legislative, judicial, and regulatory policies have combined to make America a hostile environment for worker organizing. For example, weaknesses in the National Labor Rights Act (NLRA) make it difficult for workers to place employers under sufficient stress—through demonstrations and strikes—to elicit a conciliatory response. Additionally, workers receive minimal protection under NLRA. For example, though they cannot be fired for participating in a legal strike, they can be replaced indefinitely and reinstated only at the employer's discretion—a strike deterrent equivalent to direct retribution.[112] These weaknesses are the result of deliberate political campaigns aimed at weakening workers' rights.

Increasing corporate political influence intensified union political struggles. Following a series of legislative and judicial defeats, corporations amplified their lobbying efforts between the late 1960s and early 1980s. The number of corporate political action committees quadrupled, while the number of firms with registered lobbyists leapt from 175 to 2,445.[113] The impact of this mobilization on labor interests was manifest in the defeat of the Labor Reform Act of 1977, which was intended to address some of the inadequacies of the NLRA that still plague unions today.

Since the sharp decline of union membership in the 1980s, union weakness has been exacerbated by poor enforcement of the limited protections afforded by labor laws. A 2009 study found violations in roughly half of 1,000 private-sector attempts at union certification. Coercive tactics, including threatening to cut wages, close plants, and fire workers, cut at the heart of workers' ability and right to organize and undermine even the facade of worker protection in the United States.[114]

In the face of such intimidation it would be impossible to say that new unions face a level playing field, even given the manufacturing decline. Countries facing similar declines in manufacturing have not seen comparable declines in unionization. There *is* something different about the U.S., and it is our legal and regulatory framework.

Today, thanks to outsourcing and franchising, the conventional wage-employment relationship has become rarer. Many workers officially work for a subcontractor, but in reality their relationship with the contracting company is a lot like wage employment in that it can set the terms and conditions of their work. This legal ruse has advantages for those circumventing labor regulations and taxes, but these should be seen for what they really are: exploitation of loopholes in the law to shirk responsibilities to pay overtime and a minimum wage. But legislators have failed to adapt the NLRA to these new employer–employee relationships and, by barring certain strategies,* the act prevents workers from organizing across supply chains or franchises, effectively preempting workers' rights to organize.[115]

More recently, the Supreme Court's ruling in *Harris v. Quinn* allowed workers to opt out of union dues in all states, thereby mak-

---

* Such actions include secondary action, which are strikes or protests undertaken in solidarity by employees of one firm, aimed at effecting change in a separate but related firm, and multi-employer bargaining, which is the unionization of workers across employer boundaries—a particularly effective strategy in today's fissured workplace.

ing it more difficult for unions to collect contributions for representing worker interests, and recent campaigns to expand "right to work" laws to Wisconsin, Michigan, and Indiana have sought to remove labor as a political force against conservative economic agendas in these states.[116] If this pattern continues, both U.S. workers and the American economy will suffer enormous costs.

Decline of unions threatens wages and benefits

Declining unionization has taken a toll on working families in the middle of the income distribution. Cross-country studies show that deunionization has driven a significant part of male wage inequality.[117] More recent estimates find that deunionization accounted for 20 percent of the rise in wage inequality from 1973 through 2007.[118] This deterioration is felt beyond unions themselves. Where unions pass an industry-strength threshold they contribute to pulling up standards and wages for all workers, even those in nonunion jobs.[119] As unions fade, so too does their ability to raise wages in the broader economy.

The disappearance of unions not only has had a significant impact on inequality but also threatens the health and security of a number of society's most vulnerable groups. For example, in one analysis of 15 low-wage occupations, economists at the Center for Economic and Policy Research found that unionized workers were 25 percent more likely to have health insurance and pension coverage than their non-union counterparts.[120]

The diminished political power of workers

Beyond fighting for fair working conditions, strong labor unions once functioned as a powerful conduit through which the voice of workers could be channeled into political action that checked managerial excess. This countervailing force helped ensure that the desires of the powerful few did not come to outweigh the needs of the many. Without that conduit, American workers will be left essentially voiceless.

With the political balance undermined, corporations have succeeded in the political battle to further weaken labor organizations and lower wages and labor standards. Meaningful labor reform will have to address the laws that have long suppressed worker voices in the United States.

The Sinking Floor of Labor Standards

- Stagnating workplace protections and weak enforcement have undermined middle-class workers and imperiled vulnerable low-wage workers.
- Trapped at the bottom of the income distribution, an increasing number of people are working full time but not earning enough to provide even a basic standard of living.
- Poor labor standards and enforcement have left millions of workers in poverty, generating large public social welfare costs and slowing demand.

While unionization serves as a platform on which workers can stand to push for better wages and conditions, legally mandated minimum labor standards serve as the floor on which that platform can be built. By guaranteeing minimum protections and compensation, fair labor standards help ensure the reasonable safety and financial health of America's workforce. But after years of neglect and sabotage, America's labor floor fails even to guarantee a survivable standard of living, leaving millions of U.S. workers to suffer from poverty and economic insecurity.

Beyond the direct beneficiaries, improved labor standards bolster wages and conditions across the low-wage sector as a whole and lead to a host of broader economic benefits.

Weakening standards for American workers

The structural cause of the falling labor floor is threefold. First, America's baseline standards set a very low bar for compensation and benefits relative to similar advanced-economy countries or to a baseline of basic needs. Second, the standards we do possess have failed to keep up with inflation and changes in the economy; some have been slashed. Finally, in many cases government agencies fail to enforce standards, leaving workers open to discrimination and other forms of abuse.

Our labor standards do not include health and retirement benefits, and as a result barely a third of the bottom quartile of workers receive paid sick days and only 41 percent have access to retirement benefits of any kind.[121] With no public health care option and no mandate for employers to provide it, the United States has the lowest health care coverage rate of all OECD nations although the Affordable Care Act has led to some improvement.[122]

Despite possessing the power to strengthen overtime pay, the executive branch allowed inflation to eat into overtime protections over the past 40 years while actions such as President George W. Bush's changes to overtime exemptions actually lowered the number of eligible employees. As a result, the share of full-time salaried workers receiving overtime benefits fell to just 8 percent in 2014 from 33 percent in 1980.[123]

Inflation has taken its toll on the minimum wage, too. The inflation-adjusted value of the federal minimum wage has fallen from $9.54 per hour in 1968 to $7.25 in 2014—a loss of nearly a quarter of its value.[124] And as the real value of the minimum declined, wages earned by those working at the bottom fell farther away from those earning a middle-class standard of living. As Figure 5 shows, in 2014, the minimum wage earned just 35 percent of the average U.S. wage, compared to 53 percent of the average hourly wage in the late 1960s.[125]

In other instances, labor standards have been actively weakened. Under the Bush administration, millions of employees were reclassified as independent contractors and accordingly exempted from minimum wage and overtime protections and excluded from coverage under workers' compensation laws, Social Security, unemployment insurance, Occupational Safety and Health Administration regulations, and the National Labor Relations Act.[126]

Beyond the fact that nominal standards are too low, fail-

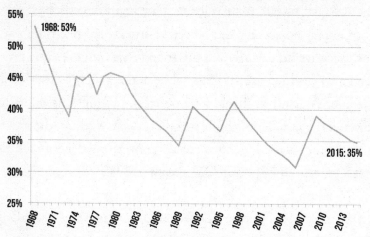

MINIMUM WAGE EARNERS FALLING FARTHER BEHIND THE AVERAGE WORKER
Federal minimum wage as a share of average hourly earnings of production workers

FIGURE 5

Source: Cooper, David, Lawrence Mishel and John Schmitt. 2015. "We Can Afford a $12.00 Federal Minimum Wage in 2020." Economic Policy Institute Briefing Paper.

ure to enforce those standards has added another layer of vulnerability to the lives of low-wage workers. Between 1980 and 2007, despite more than a 50 percent increase in the workforce, the United States cut the number of minimum wage and overtime inspectors by 31 percent. A 2008 survey of 4,000 low-wage workers in three cities found that 26 percent received less than the federal minimum wage and 76 percent did not receive overtime pay to which they were legally entitled.[127] The $1 billion of stolen wages recovered by various U.S. government agencies in 2012 suggests a widespread problem of significant magnitude, since the vast majority of wage theft goes unreported. Researchers estimated an average loss per low-wage worker of $2,634 per year with a national total of up to $50 billion per year.[128]

The roughly 8 million undocumented workers in the U.S. economy suffer disproportionately from labor law violations. Providing a pathway to citizenship for the 11 million undocumented immigrants in America will bring them out of the shadows and into formal employment protections, raising their wages along with the wages of competing naturalized citizens.[129]

Increased poverty at the low end of the labor market

Growing poverty and declining wages at the lower end of the labor market highlight how the falling labor floor contributes to inequality. In both the current and previous business cycle expansion, the poverty rate actually *increased*—an unprecedented outcome in a growth period, which suggests labor protections are perilously low and are failing to link economic growth with widespread prosperity.[130]

Beyond minimum wage earners themselves, the minimum wage appears to set the wage structure for other workers at the low end of the wage distribution. Econometric evidence indicates that changes to the minimum wage can push up or drag down wages for those just above the bottom, particularly those in the bottom 10 percent of wage earners.[131] The minimum wage also reduces poverty, with one estimate showing that a 10 percent increase in the minimum wage would reduce poverty by 2.4 percent.[132]

The minimum wage is one of the main determinants of inequality between those at the bottom of the distribution and those in the middle, often measured as the ratio of those at the 50th percentile to those at the 10th. Because the level of the minimum wage impacts wages slightly higher up the wage scale, the weakening minimum wage is one of the major reasons that inequality at the bottom has deepened in the past several decades, particularly for women and people of color.[133] Researchers at the University of California Berkeley Labor Center estimate that, because the jobs of workers at the bottom do not pay enough to meet a basic needs budget, the federal government along with taxpayers spent nearly $153 billion per year from 2009 to 2011 on Medicaid, the Children's Health Insurance Program, food stamps, and Temporary Assistance for Needy Families.[134]

Basic labor rules and standards should ensure that employers pay workers enough to provide their families at least the essentials. However, today a full-time work schedule at the minimum wage falls short of the federal poverty level for a family of two—a measure that likely understates basic need. Of all those receiving Medicaid, food stamps, TANF, or the Earned Income Tax Credit, 73 percent earn a market wage and still cannot secure a basic standard of living through labor income.[135] Beyond low wages, though, working families are suffering from uncertain work schedules and a lack of health care and retirement benefits, all of which lead to perpetuated cycles of inequality.[136]

Even within the already-vulnerable category of low-wage workers, poor labor standards hurt some groups more than others. Immigrants, women, and racial minorities are disproportionately represented among low-wage workers and precarious part-time, temporary, and informal employees. They are also the frequent target of labor standards violations.[137]

In the case of undocumented workers, research shows potential to generate growth while improving conditions. In 2013, economist Robert Lynch and immigration expert Patrick Oakford estimated that delivering comprehensive immigration reform would boost undocumented workers' wages by 15–25 percent and U.S. economic output by $832 billion to $1.4 trillion over a 10-year period.[138]

Racial Discrimination

■ Income and wealth outcomes are poor for people of color relative to whites; the disparity has grown since the financial crisis.
■ Residential and educational segregation leads to less opportunity, and employment discrimination means that getting a job is more difficult for people of color.
■ This structural discrimination creates large wealth gaps between whites and other population groups—inequalities that transmit down through generations from parents to children. This is especially troubling given that people of color make up a majority of America's future workforce.

Racial discrimination—through legalized segregation in the 19th and first half of the 20th century and through the de facto segregation and discrimination that persist today—is a clear driver of economic inequality in the United States.

Living in concentrated poverty perpetuates intergenerational cycles of wealth disparity. Radically unequal access to education, housing, and other wealth-building assets ultimately weakens the employment opportunities for African-Americans and Latinos in the United States. This inequality has an institutional basis and is not just the result of some people's personal biases. As the U.S. population becomes majority-minority by 2050, the systematic exclusion of a large swath of the population from economic opportunity will further threaten efforts to promote both equality and economic performance of the United States in an increasingly globally competitive world.[139]

A history of exclusion through rules

During the middle of the 20th century, the United States made huge public investments—in education, social services, and infrastructure—that laid the foundation for growth. The G.I. Bill, perhaps the most famous example, devoted $95 billion to help 16 million veterans returning from World War II get a college education, get job training, and purchase a home. But the benefits of such investments in the building of the middle class were never fully extended to include communities of color, and in fact they excluded African-Americans in staggering ways. To cite just one example, "by October 1, 1946, 6,500 former soldiers had been placed in nonfarm jobs by the employment service in Mississippi; 86 percent of the skilled and semiskilled jobs were filled by whites, 92 percent of the unskilled ones by blacks."[140]

Similarly, the New Deal was laden with policies that were shaped by and reinforced race and gender discrimination. For example, the projects of the Federal Housing Administration buttressed the boundaries of segregation during the Jim Crow era.[141] Agricultural and domestic workers, who were overwhelmingly African-American, were originally excluded from the Social Security program.[142] The results of decades of discrimination reverberate today.

Discrimination also extends to the housing and labor markets. Recent research has shown that across the income spectrum African-Americans, Latinos, and Asians live in higher-poverty neighborhoods than whites at similar income levels. Disparities between whites and people of color are worst at the lowest income levels. Living in neighborhoods of concentrated poverty is a phenomenon relatively common for African-Americans, Latinos, and low- and moderate-income Asians, but almost unknown for whites.[143]

Racial discrimination is also evident in policing policies and criminal justice more broadly. Currently 2.3 million Americans overall are behind bars, more than 1 percent of all adults; the incarceration rate has tripled in recent decades and is higher in absolute terms than even China's prison population.[144] Mass incarceration, which falls most heavily on populations of color, has serious consequences for economic equality as people miss out on opportunities to build human capital and face discrimination in hiring upon their release. This extends even to public schools, where African-American students are three times as likely as whites to be suspended, putting them at risk for the school-to-prison pipeline.[145]

The lack of a path to citizenship for 11.2 million undocumented Americans relegates more than 5 percent of the workforce to the shadows, vulnerable to exploitation beyond the reach of labor laws.[146] Of these, approximately 85 percent are from Mexico or other parts of Central or Latin America.[147] Undocumented status reduces bargaining power and the mobility of workers, and they are more likely to be paid lower wages for the same work and experience wage theft and labor violations because they have no enforcement mechanisms to which to turn. Undocumented workers pay taxes, though they receive a proportionally lower share of the benefits from public services, but studies show that normalizing their legal status in the workplace would raise tax revenues as well as incomes for them and other low-wage workers.[148]

Unequal outcomes for people of color

The outcomes resulting from structural discrimination that limits access to education and jobs contributes significantly to income inequality. Since the 1980s, the unemployment rate for African-Americans has averaged more than twice that for whites. While white unemployment peaked at 8.7 percent in 2010, African-American unemployment reached 16 percent. At the recession's height, white unemployment remained well below where African-American unemployment has hovered since 1980.[149]

But the problem is not unemployment alone. Even for those who do have jobs, workplace segregation persists.[150] Workers of color and especially women are disproportionately concentrated in low-wage jobs, primarily in retail, food service, and home health care.[151] Research suggests discriminatory hiring practices are in part to blame for the situation—not just lack of education.[152] In a recent field study, researchers sent similar resumes with a variety of names that sound white, African-American, or Latino to apply for entry-level, low-wage jobs in New York City. Not only were African-American applicants half as likely as equally qualified whites to get a callback or job offer, but also whites with recent prison records actually fared as well as African-American and Latino applicants with clean backgrounds and similar credentials.[153]

The outcomes of this pervasive discrimination are stark. Thirty percent of African-American children, 28 percent of Native American children, and 23 percent of Latino children live in high-poverty areas—compared to just 4 percent of white children.[154] African-Americans make up 42.5 percent of students in high-poverty elementary and secondary schools, despite accounting for less than 16 percent of the overall student population. Latino students make up nearly 31 percent of students in high-poverty schools while accounting for just 23.7 percent of the student population.[155] Because upward mobility is so dependent on education, and because the quality of the education in these poverty-ridden neighborhoods is often deficient, upward mobility for people of color is impeded.

The combination of residential and educational segregation, hiring and workplace discrimination, and undocumented status means that people of color are far more likely to end up in poverty. Poverty rates are more than double for Native Americans, African-Americans, and Latinos than they are for whites (27, 25.8, and 23.2 percent respectively, versus 11.6 percent) and the numbers are even worse for children: almost 40 percent of African-American children and more than 30 percent of Latino children live in poverty, compared to 12 percent of white children.[156]

The culmination of these structural factors keeps people of color from getting ahead in the economy. Figure 6 shows the likelihood of upward economic mobility for children born to parents in the bottom 25 percent of the income distribution. For whites born into the lowest group, 14 percent of children reached the top quarter of the income distribution as adults while 32 percent remained at the bottom. African-American children born to parents at the bottom of the income distribution were twice as likely as whites to end up there as adults; only 4 percent of African-American children from the bottom climbed to the top as adults.[157]

Institutional practices have also made it difficult for people of color to build wealth. Many banks refused to lend in neighborhoods with more than a few African-American residents. This

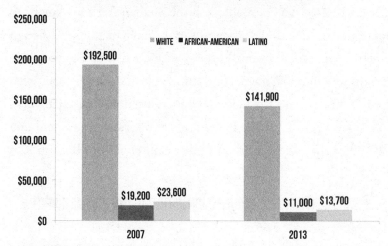

FIGURE 6

Source: Rakesh, Kochhar and Richard Fry. 2014. "Wealth Inequality has widened along racial, ethnics lines wince end of Great Recession." Pew Research.

practice, called redlining, denied African-Americans opportunities to own property and build wealth that could be passed down to their children.[158] But sadly, this policy was reinforced by government policies: Initially, the Federal Housing Administration (founded in 1934) often refused to insure mortgages in such neighborhoods.

This discrimination contributed to a self-perpetuating wealth gap: a lack of wealth makes it harder to purchase housing and build equity. A lack of wealth also makes it harder to mitigate poverty, which in turn puts people further behind in the labor market.

According to analysis of Federal Reserve data by the Pew Research Center, shown in Figure 7, the wealth gap between the median white household and the median African-American and Latino household is substantial and widening. Although median net worth over all groups decreased with the recession beginning in 2007, the decline left people of color relatively even worse off. In 2013 the median white household had a net worth 13 times that of the median African-American household and 10 times that of the median Latino household; for both groups

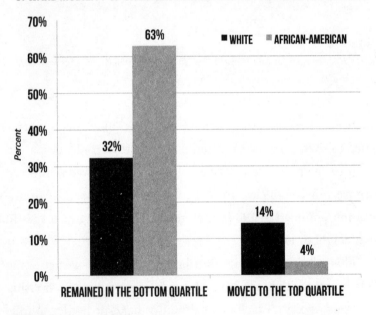

UPWARD MOBILITY OF CHILDREN BORN IN THE BOTTOM INCOME QUARTILE

FIGURE 7

Source: Hertz, Tom. 2006. "Understanding Mobility in America." Center for American Progress.

median net worth fell farther behind the median white household since the Great Recession.[159] Research shows that the largest drivers of the wealth gap are years of homeownership, household income, employment, education, and preexisting family wealth.[160] Because of the lack of inherited wealth in African-American communities, African-Americans purchase homes when they are relatively older, and thus take longer to build home equity, so they have a smaller cushion during hard financial times.[161] When the 2008 financial crisis hit, African-Americans—already economically vulnerable— were hit disproportionately hard.[162]

Because incarceration or formerly incarcerated status affects employment, earnings, and economic mobility, it increases poverty for individuals and families, but disproportionately for people of color: 2.3 percent of African-Americans and 0.7 percent of Latinos are incarcerated, compared to 0.4 percent of whites.[163] According to a 2010 Pew Charitable Trust report, incarceration "reduces hourly wages for men by approximately 11 percent, annual employment by 9 weeks, and annual earnings by 40 percent."[164]

The effects of incarceration transcend an inmate's time within the correctional system and have lifelong, even intergenerational impacts on economic productivity. Indeed, many scholars, including Michelle Alexander, view the prevalence of criminal records as a modern "Jim Crow," banishing African-Americans to second-class status over multiple generations.[165]

Those with a criminal record have significant difficulty

finding a job for any number of reasons, including laws that prevent them from working in certain occupations and potential legal liabilities pertaining to employers, plus they are denied access to important social safety nets like education and housing.[166] The American Bar Association uncovered 38,000 statutes with a collateral consequence for a conviction; 84 percent of these are related to employment, and 82 percent of them have no end date. The ABA notes that "a crime committed at age 18 can ostensibly deny a former offender the ability to be a licensed barber or stylist when he or she is 65 years old."[167]

The economic consequences of structural discrimination

Taking into account both the increasingly punitive nature of the criminal justice system and labor market discrimination, leading to higher unemployment rates—especially in the Great Recession—and lower wages, most African-American men are in no better of a position relative to white men than they were in the late 1960s.[168]

In addition to the cost of discrimination for individuals and their communities, structural discrimination serves as a drag on national economic performance. There are many estimates of the costs of discrimination for African-Americans, including the aggregate loss of not using existing and potential education and skills. Chris Benner and Manuel Pastor examined factors that could explain "growth spells" for the 184 biggest U.S. regions from 1990 to 2011, and they found that the duration of these growth spells was strongly connected to income inequality and racial segregation. "The punch line of this work is that regions that are more equal and more integrated—across income, race, and place—are better able to sustain growth over time."[169]

In sum, a combination of historical exclusion, segregation, and discrimination has led to markedly worse economic outcomes for people of color relative to whites. And children disproportionately bear the brunt, which is not only morally reprehensible but also economically unsound and bad for growth. But this is a call to action rather than despair: even the most pernicious effects of race and class discrimination can be battled with better policy decisions.

Gender Discrimination

■ Labor institutions and government policy create obstacles to women joining the workforce.
■ Women face structural discrimination that increases inequality.
■ Discrimination in wages and access to work reduces aggregate demand and hampers growth.

The entrance of women into the workforce since the 1970s has had profound effects on economic performance. Between 1950 and 1999, the workforce participation rate for women 15 and over rose from less than 40 percent to 60 percent. Women's entrance into the workforce in the 1970s and 1980s drove nearly a fifth of real GDP growth.[170]

However, U.S. labor market institutions designed to support the two-parent, one-income households of the 1950s have failed to adapt to the new reality. Gender discrimination at the workplace, as well as factors such as a lack of paid sick and family leave and the unavailability of affordable childcare, have dampened women's incentives to participate in the labor force. Women's workforce participation is well below its potential, particularly in the U.S. Indeed, over the past 15 years, women's participation in the U.S. labor force has declined from 77 percent to 74 percent for prime-age workers, while participation in the labor force has increased for women in most other advanced economy countries.[171]

The rules fail to accommodate working women

Lack of pregnancy and maternity protections often drive women out of the workforce. Among working mothers without paid leave who lost their jobs after staying home with a newborn, less than half found jobs again within a year. By contrast, 87.4 percent of mothers with paid family leave returned to work within a year.[172]

Women who participate in the workforce face significant hurdles. They comprise two-thirds of the nearly 20 million low-wage workers in the country, even though they represent less than half of all workers. Half of the women working in low-wage jobs are women of color. Mothers make up 3.5 times as large a share of the low-wage workforce as do fathers (21 percent vs. 6 percent).[173]

Meanwhile, occupations considered predominately female— namely nursing, home health care, and educational services— remain undercompensated.[174] Recent studies reveal that regardless of gender or skill level, workers in these female-dominated fields earn less than their equivalents employed outside the "caring economy."[175]

A lack of family-friendly policies keeps many women out of the workforce and makes it harder for those who are working to balance the demands of juggling work, family, and social responsibilities. A mere 13 percent of U.S. workers have employer-based paid family leave, nearly two-in-five private-sector workers (roughly 40 million people) lack even a single paid sick day, and fewer than 40 percent have access to personal medical leave through employer-provided short-term disability insurance.[176] Ninety-five percent of part-time and low-wage workers have no access to paid family leave.[177] A 2013 Oxfam survey found that 14 percent of low-wage workers had lost a job in the previous four years due to their own or a family member's illness.[178]

The impact of paid leave policy can be seen in the differences in women's labor force participation across a selection of advanced-economy countries (Figure 8). In the United States, with no paid leave policy, only 74 percent of working-age women participated in the labor force in 2013—the same rate as in 1990. Contrast this with other peer countries, where paid leave benefits start at 26 weeks and often extend to both parents, and where

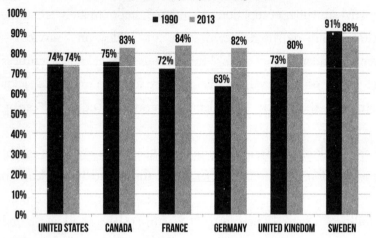

FIGURE 8

Source: Authors' analysis: "Online OECD Employment Database." Organization for Economic Development.

smart policies have empowered women to balance work and family life, enabling more to participate in work and contributing to the overall economy.[179] In each of these countries today, more than 80 percent of women aged 25–54 are in the labor force.

Reproductive health care is a matter of economic security. In one study that asked women why they use birth control, the majority reported that doing so allowed them to take better care of themselves or their families, support themselves financially, get or keep a job, or complete their education.[180] Research has shown that women's ability to plan and space their pregnancies (through access to birth control) improves educational attainment and lifetime earnings.[181] Other studies have shown the multigenerational impacts of family planning access: When mothers have access to birth control, their children are more likely to have higher family incomes and college completion rates.[182] Even though the Affordable Care Act has dramatically improved the standard of care guaranteed to women who have insurance coverage, recent restrictions on abortion and family planning have made it more difficult for all women to access comprehensive health care.[183] These restrictions lead not only to a series of devastating health consequences, but contribute to the economic insecurity of women and their entire families and communities.

The enduring gender pay gap

The wages of U.S. women continue to lag behind those of their male counterparts of equal age, education, and professional experience, more than 50 years ago President John F. Kennedy signed the Equal Pay Act, which prohibits discrimination "on account of sex in the payment of wages by employers." At that time, women were paid 59 cents for every dollar paid to their male counterparts. A half-century has passed and that gap has shrunk by less than 20 cents; women today make approximately 78 cents for every dollar paid to their male counterparts. African-American and Latina women are paid only 64 and 56 cents, respectively, for every dollar paid to white men, equivalent to an annual loss of nearly $19,000 for African-American women and $23,279 for Latinas.[184]

Economic benefits of gender equality

Addressing these economic and health inequities is not only a moral necessity, but would also have significant economic benefits, both for families and for the economy more broadly. Implementing equal pay would mean an income increase for nearly 60 percent of U.S. women. Two-thirds of single mothers would get a raise of 17 percent (equal to more than $6,000 a year), and the poverty rate among these families would drop from 28.7 percent to 15 percent. Pay equity would reduce poverty among working women by half and would therefore reduce the need for the safety net programs many working families rely on to make ends meet. The total increase in women's earnings as a result of pay equity would be 14 times greater than combined federal and state expenditures on Temporary Assistance for Needy Families.[185]

Continued discrimination against women in the workforce increases economic inequality, but also reduces aggregate demand and thereby stymies economic performance. Raising women's labor force participation rate to that of men's has been a huge boon to economic performance across nations—a truly meaningful "supply side" measure. Doing so would increase U.S. GDP by 5 percent.[186] Paying women the same wage as men for equal work would increase U.S. GDP by 3–4 percentage points, according to recent estimates.[187] Considering that the incentive of equal pay would further increase women's workforce participation, the stimulus impact may be even bigger.

REWRITING THE RULES

To fix the economy for average Americans, we need to tackle the rules and institutions that have generated low investment, sluggish growth, and runaway incomes and wealth accumulation at the top and created a steeper hill for the rest to climb. It would be easier, politically, to push for one or two policies on which we have consensus, but that approach would be insufficient to match the severity of the problems posed by rising inequality. This set of proposals aims to reduce inequality and improve economic performance by restructuring the rules shaping the economy. As we discussed in the previous section, we cannot alter the dynamics of our distorted economy without broad, bold, and comprehensive measures to put the United States back on track.

The agenda we offer pulls apart the web of privileges and incentives business lobbyists and their politicians have woven into the rules of the economy and our society—and which have led businesses away from the kind of productive investments that would lead to robust and broadly shared economic performance. The policy reforms we envision would restructure how businesses, employees, and the public sector work together to ensure that work delivers a good standard of living and that we make the investments needed for the U.S. economy to thrive and face the challenges of a globally competitive world.

The approach is twofold. The first move is to tame rent-seeking behaviors that unduly reward those at the top while raising costs for the rest and reducing the efficiency and stability of the U.S. economy. As long as the growth of the economy is predicated on rent-seeking and financial bubbles, we will not see the investment in companies, people, and infrastructure needed for sustainable growth. We begin by looking at the markets where firms have outsized power—both to make rules and to extract rents—and aim to reset the rules so that these markets will function more productively. Next, we examine the financial sector, which for years has had the power to regulate itself and evade public scrutiny, and we seek to ensure that it fulfills its societal missions without imposing excess costs on the rest of society. We also seek to address rampant short-termism, which has supplanted productive long-term corporate health. Finally, we outline tax reform that would reduce rent-seeking incentives and raise revenue for public investment.

The second part of our agenda seeks to restore the rules and institutions that ensure security and opportunity for the middle class. The steps along this path are straightforward: Restore full employment and invest in public infrastructure. Update and enforce the rules that protect workers to ensure wages keep pace with productivity. Reduce obstacles to labor market participation for all workers, particularly women, people of color, and immigrants. Finally, provide affordable and quality public education, health care, childcare, and financial services, as well as retirement security, to enable families and individuals—all Americans—to pursue the American dream through work. To compete globally in the 21st century, the U.S. economy needs to have every cylinder firing.

Some of these ideas are new and some are familiar, but they all build on renewing the promise of security, opportunity, and freedom from want that America made 75 years ago as it emerged from the Great Depression and established itself as the world's preeminent power. The New Deal created a baseline of innovative policies committed to economic growth, opportunity for all, and protection of those less able to fend for themselves. President Franklin Roosevelt developed institutions to balance government and the private sector in pursuit of both growth and the common good. The New Deal set the standard for large reductions in inequality and huge economic gains for several generations that followed.

The inequality we are experiencing is a choice, and we have the opportunity to make a better choice. Generations still to come will be grateful if we can deliver on President Roosevelt's commitment.

TAMING THE TOP

The growth of the top 1 percent was enabled by specific policy decisions. It occurred when we removed safeguards that protected consumers and taxpayers from excesses in the financial industry and failed to update other common-sense regulations. It occurred when corporations cast aside their own long-term interests in favor of short-term stock gains for shareholders and distortionary CEO pay packages. It occurred when we restructured the tax code in ways that led to more leverage and higher executive pay, as opposed to more investment in productive assets. Addressing these issues doesn't just address inequality; doing so will also build a solid foundation for the economy of the 21st century.

To secure the investments needed for future growth and shared prosperity, we must circumscribe market power, fix the financial sector, incentivize long-term corporate management, and rebalance the tax code. An agenda to do so is outlined below.

Make Markets Competitive

Inequality is exacerbated by power—deviations of the market economy from the competitive paradigm. In many sectors, firms have had the power to raise prices. There is not just market power, in the sense that the term is usually understood. There is also political power—the ability of corporations to secure legislation and regulations that enable them to charge more to consumers and to pay less to suppliers and workers, to get more from the government while contributing less to the public good. President Theodore Roosevelt used antitrust laws to curb both the economic *and* political power of the large corporations. The economy has evolved, but antitrust has not always kept up. It has failed to attack monopoly and monopsony power in all the manifestations that have become endemic in the 21st century.

We need a 21st century competition law that recognizes that we have moved from a manufacturing to a service and knowledge economy, where different principles of competition are relevant. Below we propose interventions to restore balance in a few key areas: intellectual property rights, global trade agreements, health care prices, and consumer finance protections. However, many of the proposals outlined in later sections— from the financial sector and labor law to monetary policy to the management of globalization—also aim to rebalance a network of rules and institutions that have increasingly exacerbated the imbalances of political and economic power in the country.

Restore balance to intellectual property rights

Intellectual property rights, or IPRs, provide a clear example of how markets cannot be separated from the human-made rules that shape them. A legal framework and supporting institutions must provide appropriate incentives for innovation and encourage investment. But incentives must be balanced with the imperative for innovations and the associated knowledge to be widely dispersed and accessible in the interest of fair competition. IPRs can be written to achieve this balance, but our intellectual property regime has lost its sense of balance, with consequences that can be dramatic.

Today in the U.S., IPRs often shield intellectual property owners from competition in the same way high tariffs protect domestic industries. They raise prices paid by consumers, with the additional payments generating monopoly profits. In one example, the grant to the company Myriad of the patents to BRCA genes—the genes that affect the likelihood of getting breast cancer—impeded access to life-saving tests and the development of cheaper and more effective tests. After the Supreme Court in a pathbreaking ruling invalidated the patent protection, far better and cheaper tests emerged. But the legacy of Myriad's market power, created by its patent, lives on; it still has the lion's share of the market.

In trade agreements like the Trans-Pacific Partnership, the United States pushes strong IPRs without balance, which advances the interests of the pharmaceutical, software, and entertainment industries but does not yield the most economic benefits or—the evidence shows—provide meaningful incentives for innovators. Insistence on including excessively stringent IPR protections would mean that life-saving medicines, renewable energy technologies, and other innovations are put further out of reach both in the United States and in trading-partner countries, deterring more research and development and undermining health and the environment.

Better balance is possible. For instance, in the United States, we balanced the need for innovation and access to life-saving drugs with the Hatch-Waxman Act of 1984, making lower-cost generic drugs leap to 86 percent of all drugs dispensed in pharmacies and health care facilities from 19 percent at the time of the bill.[1] Without competition from generics, drug prices would be even higher than they are today.

Restore balance to global trade agreements

While it is essential that the United States work with global partners to establish rules for international trade and investment, the kinds of rules that we've been making through trade agreements increasingly set the terms of trade in favor of businesses and against workers and the public interest in both the United States and among our economic partners. These rules determine who will benefit from an increasingly globalized world, but trade agreements—written behind closed doors, with the active participation of firms but no other stakeholders—are failing to deliver the rules we need for managing globalization in a way that benefits all.

One set of provisions that increasingly balances the odds against ordinary Americans is the protections for investors that U.S. negotiators insist other countries must adopt in the so-called investor-state dispute settlement mechanisms. These provisions create private international arbitration panels in which investors can sue governments, and parties have no recourse to legal review and appeal. While investors should be protected against rogue governments seizing their assets or formulating policies that discriminate against specific firms, this is not what these provisions are about; investors can already buy insurance against such outcomes from the World Bank's Multilateral Investment Guarantee Agency as well as some U.S. government programs for insuring investment. Rather, the real intent of these provisions is to impede health, environmental, consumer safety, and even financial regulations meant to protect the public interest from egregious business practices. That's why U.S. negotiators insisted on including such investor protections in an agreement with the European Union—where the rule of law and protections against expropriation are already on par with the United States. By limiting the scope for policy in the public interest, investor protections actually make it harder for trading-partner countries to raise their own standards and make it easier for companies to move production offshore or extract wage concessions with such threats.

Trade agreements with true high-road standards for the global economy—be they in labor rights or environmental, consumer, and public health protections—would have rules where the benefits of an agreement are only made available contingent on certified compliance with standards. In other words, businesses wishing to trade with businesses in the United States under the terms of an agreement should be audited and certified by a credible, independent third party such as the International Labor Organization; certification then buys the company a right to trade under the preferential treatment of a trade agreement. This requirement has been shown to work to raise standards—for example, among Cambodian garment exporters—in contrast to the enforcement model of other U.S. agreements covering trade from Bahrain to Bogota on which the Trans-Pacific Partnership is based.[2]

Getting the rules right on trade begins by not exporting to other countries the economic rules that have led to skyrocketing inequality in income, wealth, and political influence. While much of the "trade policy" agenda focuses on technical legal aspects of international economics, we also know that international agreements don't create trade, people do. Policies outlined elsewhere in this report aiming to establish true equality of opportunity and to tame the excesses of market power for a more open and broadly beneficial market competition will also be key to ensuring that people in the U.S. economy can seize on and create the opportunities made possible by a world with deepening globalization.

Control health care cost by allowing government bargaining

Firms across the health care industry, from hospitals to insurance companies to drug makers, have been allowed to consolidate and expand, reducing competition and thus raising prices. Additionally, government has legally circumscribed our own ability to negotiate costs. Indeed, U.S. health care costs are the highest in the world—we spend more (both absolutely and as a percentage of GDP) than any other country, and yet outcomes are disappointing, far poorer than many countries that spend significantly less.[3] By bargaining with drug companies for bulk purchases, the U.S. Department of Veterans Affairs pays 40 percent lower prices for prescription drugs than typical market prices.[4] In contrast, the 2003 Medicare Part D expansion explicitly prohibited negotiating for lower drug prices, meaning senior citizens and taxpayers pay significantly more for drugs.[5] The federal government should establish a national prescription drug formulary, establishing the cost effectiveness for all prescription purchases covered under all public health insurance plans, not just those for veterans. Competition to be one of the recommended medicines on the formulary—with a high benefit cost ratio—will drive down prices.

Rebalance the rules for bankruptcy by expanding coverage to homeowners and students

When individuals or corporations can't repay what is owed, a bargaining process usually follows. The legal backdrop—what happens if the parties can't reach an agreement—determines the relative bargaining power of the different creditors and the debtor, and shapes the outcome of the bargaining process. Changing the rules to favor creditors—as we did in the so-called Bankruptcy Abuse Prevention and Consumer Protection Act of

2005—provides a clear example of how the legal and institutional framework shapes the economy and increases inequality. While we did not circumscribe practices like predatory lending or usurious interest rates that ultimately led to situations where large numbers of Americans became overindebted, we did strengthen the bargaining power of banks.

Similarly, current bankruptcy laws favor certain sets of debtors and lenders over others. We changed the bankruptcy laws to prioritize repayment on derivatives—the nontransparent financial products from which the banks make so much money and which contributed so much to the 2008 financial crisis—over repayment of debts to workers. At the same time we made student debt more difficult to discharge than loans taken to buy a yacht.

Simply reversing these changes would be a start in restoring balance. Removing the special protections for derivatives in bankruptcy, a feature that benefits Wall Street but actually makes firms more risky as they rely more on these exotic instruments, is essential in reducing the excessive financialization of the economy. Removing some of the most burdensome elements designed to make filing for bankruptcy harder will help individuals move on from the misfortunes that can happen throughout life. Of course, a large fraction of personal bankruptcies in recent years has been a result of a medical emergency, an extended period of unemployment, and especially a combination of the two.[6] The health care reforms already enacted and the reforms in macroeconomic policy discussed below—combined with curbing the predatory and exploitive activities of the financial sector—should make the occurrence of bankruptcy and financial hardship more rare.

But there is more we can do. A homeowners' chapter 11, analogous to corporate chapter 11, would keep families in homes and give a fresh start to families overburdened with debt.

Fix the Financial Sector

A recurrent theme of this report is that the financial sector has not been performing the tasks that it is supposed to: managing risk, allocating capital efficiently, intermediating between savers and investors, providing funds for investments and job creation, and running an efficient 21st century payments mechanism. Rather, it has mismanaged risk, misallocated capital, prioritized exploitation and market manipulation, and created an extraordinarily expensive payments mechanism, out of tune with the advances afforded by modern technology. A well-functioning economy needs to have a well-functioning financial market. Financial markets are important. Unfortunately, our financial market, while not performing the critical tasks of providing capital to worthy endeavors, has given rise to enormous inequalities and has resulted in poorer economic performance—lower growth and more instability.

As a result, the economy is weaker and more prone to bubbles and panics. The Dodd-Frank Act was a start, but the legislation did not change the structure of the dysfunctional system. Further reform can and should reduce the risks of the financial sector to the economy as a whole, increase transparency, combat short-term time horizons, enhance competition, reduce the scope for rent-seeking, and make sure that banks fulfill their primary social responsibility of providing the financing that firms need to invest and innovate.

The goal of the financial sector reforms we propose are two-fold. First, we aim to prevent the sector from imposing *harm* on the rest of society, either on individuals (as evidenced in predatory lending and market manipulation) or on the economy as a whole (through the systemic effects cascading from individually reckless financial behaviors).

Second, we aim to develop a financial system that actually serves our society—for instance by helping to effectively finance small business, education, and housing. If the middle-class life is to be attainable for all, we will have to have financial products and a financial system that supports its flourishing. It is regrettable that almost all of the discussions of reforming the financial sector have focused on the first goal—simply preventing harm. Taking away opportunities for high profits from antisocial activities holds out the promise that the sector might refocus its attention on what it is supposed to be doing. But there is more that can be done, and in later sections, we provide examples.

In this section we focus on the first goal: curbing the current system's risks to the overall economy and curtailing practices that directly cost consumers. We propose an agenda that ends "too big to fail," reduces the risks in "shadow banking," increases financial market transparency, makes a more efficient payments mechanism by limiting credit and debit card fees and enhancing competition, enforces rules with stricter penalties, and reforms Federal Reserve governance. Later in the report we will outline plans to improve financing of essential elements of a successful life, like paying for a college education or buying a home.

End "too big to fail"

We have yet to undertake the reforms needed to end too big to fail and thus reduce the potential for failure of large financial institutions to damage the broader economy. Banks that are backed by the government and are so big that their failure will cause the entire economy to contract don't need to internalize the costs of their failures and can reap huge benefits from risky bets. They have a perverse incentive to take on excess risk, knowing that should a problem arise they will be bailed out, with losses being borne by others. This, of course, is exactly what occurred in the 2008 financial crisis, the impacts of which still reverberate throughout the economy.

Despite recent experience and the Dodd-Frank reform, banks are still not only too big to fail, but also too big to manage—evidenced by repeated failures like the "London Whale."*

---

* The so-called "London Whale" refers to a trader (or a group of traders) at the JP Morgan London office who lost more than $6 billion for the bank in a series of risky derivatives bets over the course of 2012. The incident highlighted lacking oversight both internally and on the part of regulators.

And even when they are not too big to fail, they can be too interconnected, too interlinked to fail: with excessive linkages (e.g., those associated with CDs and derivatives), the failure of one institution can lead to a cascade of other failures—stoppable only with a government bailout. That is why interlinkages need to be transparent and regulated.

The Financial Stability Oversight Council should assess large, systemically risky financial firms with an additional capital surcharge above what regulators currently assess under the Basel Accords in order to make failure less likely and more manageable. Moreover, being too big to fail (or too interconnected to fail) gives banks an advantage: they don't have to account for the costs their failure poses to the system as a whole, and get a subsidy as a result. The surcharge corrects for a market distortion that otherwise would favor such banks, even if they are not more efficient than smaller ones.

A surcharge would force banks to internalize the true cost of their risks and improve economic efficiency, while insulating taxpayers from the costs of failed institutions. And, to avoid the unproductive debate over how to exactly quantify "systemically important financial institutions," the requirements should be graduated rather than set to a specific level.

Further, if firms are incapable of producing "living wills" that the Federal Reserve and the Federal Deposit Insurance Corporation believe show how they can unwind in bankruptcy without causing massive costs to the rest of the economy, then these institutions need to be broken up along business lines and by size so that potential failures can be better managed. In addition, living wills and their analyses should be made public. The wills have to be designed to work not just in normal times but also in the abnormal times associated with a financial crisis. Some doubt whether meaningful living wills can in fact be constructed, given the kind of turmoil that can arise in the midst of a crisis. If this is the case, then the only recourse is to begin the process of breaking up the too big to fail institutions in the same way we once broke up Standard Oil and AT&T.

Regulate the shadow banking sector and end offshore banking

Among the too-big-to-fail financial institutions are shadow banks, which are nonbank financial institutions that engage in lending by trading bonds and securities, often by bundling them through a process called securitization. They include money market funds, insurance companies like AIG, and even automakers. Even though these nonbank financial institutions were integral to the causes of the financial crisis, with many of them having to be bailed out, post-crisis reform hasn't done enough to address the enormous risks inherent in the sector's opaque activities and non-arms-length lending.

The shadow banking sector continues to grow while remaining insufficiently regulated.[7] In fact, much of the activity in the shadow banking system is motivated not by its greater efficiency but simply to circumvent regulations designed to ensure the stability and efficiency of the financial system. We must not only address the regulatory defects that have allowed this sector to grow too fast. The crisis revealed that our regulatory structure was not up to the task; it hadn't adapted to the new ways that credit was provided within the shadow banking system. But by general consensus, in the aftermath of the crisis, the shadow banking system continues to be inadequately regulated. It is a matter of choice that we have failed.

For instance, regulation should improve transparency in the entities considered shadow banks. As just one example of how to increase transparency, the Securities and Exchange Commission should reevaluate and expand on its recent ruling on money market mutual funds, whose vulnerabilities in the 2008 financial crisis sparked a panic. The ruling required that all money market mutual funds be valued on a floating basis reflecting the value of their underlying assets, rather than a fixed price of $1 per share. A good expansion would be to apply the floating values rule to all money funds. This rule would help shore up money market risk, and in particular, reduce the likelihood of panics.[8]

We also need to clarify the government's role as a lender to these nonbank financial institutions. The current ambiguity increases overall risk. During the 2008 financial crisis, the Federal Reserve radically expanded its ability to function as a lender of last resort and provided liquidity services to the shadow-banking sector, thus expanding the too-big-to-fail subsidy to an even broader set of institutions. Emergency lending is crucial in a crisis, and is one of the powers the federal government has to help mitigate the risk of a financial panic. But without clear rules, guidelines, and limits, these powers can become subject to serious abuse. As a result, Congress, under the Dodd-Frank Act, requires the Federal Reserve to only establish an "emergency lending program or facility [that] is for the purpose of providing liquidity to the financial system, and not to aid a failing financial company" in a crisis. The Fed was required to establish clear procedures to meet that goal but has dragged its feet, writing a weak rule that insufficiently clarifies its role.[9] The Federal Reserve must write clear rules outlining the government's role in back-stopping the shadow banks. It must ensure the regulatory framework is sufficiently strong that such back-stopping is truly a rare event and it must impose charges on the shadow banking system for the costs imposed on society and the risk of potential bailout costs. Congress should take action if the Federal Reserve makes no progress in writing these rules.

Most importantly, there needs to be a re-examination of the extent to which shadow banks and offshore financial centers are used to end-run the regulations designed to ensure a safe and sound financial system. It is hard to understand what true economic advantages—other than regulatory circumvention—Cayman Islands or other offshore banking centers have over those located onshore. The U.S. has the requisite financial expertise—indeed, much of the management of the offshore accounts is actually done in the U.S.[10]

Bring transparency to all financial markets

Opaque activities in finance are not limited to credit intermediation. The uncompetitive and often undisclosed fees associated with asset management, particularly those from alternative
management vehicles like private equity funds and hedge funds,
are a driving source of financial sector growth, profits in that
sector, and the income share of the top 1 percent.[11] Furthermore, most investors in IRAs and other financial products don't
understand the rules under which they operate—that the managers of such funds are not even held to a fiduciary standard and
can be conflicted. Of course, any excess fee is simply a transfer
of wealth from regular investors in these pension funds or savings vehicles to those in the financial sector.

Already, thanks to a provision of Dodd-Frank that requires
private equity to register with the SEC, significant amounts
of fraud or substandard behavior have been disclosed. As the
director of the SEC's Office of Compliance Inspections and
Examinations put it after investigating a sample of 150 newly
registered private equity advisers: "we have identified what we
believe are violations of law or material weaknesses in controls
over 50 percent of the time."[12] Congress should expand the
SEC's mission, and require private equity and hedge funds to
disclose holdings, returns, and fee structures. The SEC should
provide additional regulatory scrutiny and investor advice on
these deals. This will formalize their regulation, making it similar to mutual fund regulations; the competition that will follow

from this price transparency will help reduce financial rents. (Later, we discuss further reforms to help protect those saving for retirement.)

Reduce credit and debit card fees

High consumer fees on credit and debit card transactions are one clear symptom of abuse of market power in the financial sector. Modern technology should enable the transfer of money from an individual's bank account to that of the merchant from whom he or she is making a purchase to cost but a fraction of cent. Instead, the fees credit and debit card companies charge merchants—often 1–3 percent or more of the cost of the transaction—do not reflect the cost of services provided but rather a monopoly rent on the country's networked payments infrastructure. Ironically, financial institutions often lobby against taxes that increase transaction costs at far lower rates by arguing that the added fee will hurt business.

The Durbin amendment to the Dodd-Frank bill was supposed to bring down the excessive fees that the debit card companies impose on merchants (and which are passed along to consumers in the form of higher prices). Increased prices from monopoly power, as we noted, are just as important in lowering standards of living for ordinary Americans as decreased nominal wages. But Dodd-Frank delegated responsibility for the implementation of the regulation to the Federal Reserve, which has not sufficiently reduced the fees. Further, the Durbin amend-

ment was limited to debit cards, leaving the even more important credit card market open to unrestrained monopoly power.
Recent court decisions hold open the promise that the market
will be more competitive in the future, but we should not rely on
this. We need to make sure that the market acts competitively,
and that the financial sector does not exploit its market power
over the payments mechanism.

Enforce rules with stricter penalties

The enforcement of the rules is just as important as the rules
themselves. And in the past decade there's been a shift away
from strict criminal enforcement of financial regulation.
Fewer, if any, cases go to court. Instead the SEC and the Justice
Department settle with favorable conditions, such as deferred
prosecution agreements. Under these agreements, the parties
regularly don't admit to any wrongdoing, or even pay penalties
commensurate to their benefits. No individual is held directly
accountable. The fines that are paid come from shareholders
and are tax deductible; the perpetrators of the offenses aren't
necessarily punished or made to give back the compensation
they received as a reward for the extra profits generated by their
illegal activities.[13] Enforcement has swung toward these favorable deals instead of serious consequences and convictions for
wrongdoing.

The firms promise not to engage in the proscribed activity
(which they have not admitted doing), but then they are repeat-

edly hauled up for engaging in similar activities. It is clear that the kind of enforcement we have is not acting as a sufficient deterrent.

The SEC and other regulatory agencies should instead focus on more strict enforcement, and Congress should hold the agencies accountable if no progress is made. No company should be able to enter into a deal like a deferred prosecution agreement if it is already operating under such an agreement. These agreements should face stricter judicial review and scrutiny. And compensation schemes should be designed so that perpetrators face significant consequences—for instance, a clawback of bonuses and a reduction in retirement benefits.

Reform Federal Reserve governance

The mindset of who enforces these rules also matters. Many of the regulations in the financial sector are enforced by the Federal Reserve. And the leadership at the Federal Reserve is too often influenced by the largest financial interests rather than by small lenders and borrows. Reforms to the governance structure of the Fed should focus on reducing the conflicts of interest that seem so apparent and reforming the process by which officials are chosen.

Concern about the Fed's behavior has focused mostly on its conduct of monetary policy and the management of the 2008 bailout.

On the right, many argue for a rules-based system—monetarism, under the influence of Milton Friedman, called for the money supply to increase at a fixed rate. But the evolving structure of the economy largely discredited such theories and their ability to ensure the macro-stability of the economy. On the left, there was a concern that the Federal Reserve reflected more the interests of financial markets, with their focus on inflation, than the economy as a whole, or workers in particular, who were more concerned with unemployment. Even officials who did not come from Wall Street appeared to be "cognitively captured." These issues received heightened attention in the aftermath of the 2008 crisis, when the Federal Reserve appeared unwilling to disclose many details of what it, together with the Treasury, had done. Among the beneficiaries of the largesse were the institutions whose executives had served on the committees selecting the head of the New York Fed. And numerous reports raised questions about the appropriateness of Fed actions, many of which reflected de facto subsidies, of enormous proportions, to certain institutions. The Fed is a *public* institution; it has been given public responsibilities in the macro-management of the economy, the conduct of bailouts, and the regulation of the financial system and the governance of the Fed should reflect this.

A 2011 study by the Government Accountability Office found significant scope for improvement in management of conflict of interest within the Fed system.[14] Employees and members of all the regional boards of the Fed should be required to disclose all *potential* conflicts of interest (defining that very broadly); individuals with any significant conflict of interest should be precluded from employment or membership in the board of any regional Fed; members should be required to recuse themselves from decision making in cases with any possible conflict of interest; and members should be held to a revolving-door agreement that prevents working for the financial industry for some time after their term of service. On top of this, the boards and officers of regional Federal Reserve banks should be chosen in transparent and accountable elections.

Incentivize Long-Term Business Growth

Short-termism is not just a major problem for our corporations; it's a problem for the economy overall. Previously, we explained how the rules governing corporations and taxes on capital and top incomes have changed to favor short-term shareholders and CEOs who chase short-term stock price gains above all else. Not only have the resulting changes in behavior led to greater inequality, but the short-termism undermines real investments that create the potential for long-term economic growth. Short-termism distorts our economy, leading to lower investment, including in our workers, and weak job creation.

We propose an agenda that will incentivize corporate investment in capital equipment, research and development, and workforce development, thereby increasing economic dynamism and innovation. To do so we must realign CEO pay incentives, enact a financial transaction tax to curb short-term trading, and empower longer-term stakeholders.

Restructure CEO pay

Earlier, we explained how executive pay does not provide the desirable incentives that its advocates claim, but that stock options actually *distort* incentives—including the distortions so evident in "creative accounting" that contribute to the misallocation of capital.[15] It also has a crucial effect on inequality in the economy as a whole. When CEO pay is sky-high, it then creates social norms that drive up the salaries of executives at non-profits and other institutions, exacerbating inequality further.

The easiest way to begin addressing executive pay is to adjust the tax code, which privileges compensation of executives through equity-heavy compensation, particularly stock options. Eliminating or curtailing the performance-pay loophole (by which stock options and other excessive CEO pay receives favorable treatment) not only would help address executive pay, it would also discourage CEOs from behaving like financial speculators. Congress should maintain the current $1 million cap on the deductibility of executive compensation reform and eliminate the exception for so-called performance pay; these limits on deductibility should also be expanded to the highest paid executives in a company overall.*

There are other steps that government can and should take.

---

* Changes to deductibility of performance pay should also be expanded out from public companies to all companies that have quarterly filing with the SEC.

There needs to be more transparency in executive compensation. There should be strong disclosure requirements concerning the dilution of shareholder value as a result of stock options. And there needs to be better, more transparent reporting of the full value of executive compensation for each corporation. Current reporting of compensation packages is often opaque with the value buried in the complexities of stock option issuance and only disclosed in hard-to-interpret footnotes. The SEC should require corporations to state the value of compensation in simple, easy to understand language.

Shareholders should have a say in the pay that the companies they supposedly "own" give to their executives. There should be mandatory shareholder votes on executive compensation on an annual basis.* With so many boards of directors stacked with friends of the management—and often with CEOs from other companies, who know their pay will go up if that of other firms increases—the boards cannot be expected to provide a check against exorbitant compensation. A further proposal would peg corporate tax rates to the ratio of CEO pay to median worker pay (or even to the minimum pay)—with a tax on any excess. Of course, this would depend on the SEC finally implementing the CEO-to-worker pay-ratio disclosure rule. Alternatively, corporations with good governance that did not pay their top management excessively could be taxed at a lower rate.

---

* Our current Say-on-Pay rule is non-binding.

Enact a financial transactions tax

Short-term financial transactions can contribute to economic volatility without providing any larger benefit to the economy as a whole. These transactions also point the financial markets toward a short-term focus over the interests of longer-term shareholders and stakeholders. A financial transaction tax would penalize short-term traders and incentivize longer holding periods, thus reducing instability and encouraging longer-term productive investment. Further, a financial transaction tax even at very low rates would raise considerable revenue.[16]

Before 1975 the financial sector charged a fixed brokerage commission on trades that, for consumers, functioned like a tax. There is little evidence that the elimination of this fee improved financial markets, and a variant of financial transaction taxes are currently employed without negative consequence in vibrant financial centers like London and Hong Kong, so there is little reason to believe that a tax on transactions would present a major disruption.[17] Further, in the U.S. many brokerage houses and investment firms charge high transaction costs to consumers and have fought regulations that would reduce these costs— for example on managing retirement accounts. The difference, of course, is to whom the cost accrues. For the average investor in a 401(k), a financial transaction tax would present a minimal expense.[18] Congress should pass a financial transaction tax designed to encourage productive investment.[19]

Empower long-term stakeholders

The current tax code plays a role in incentivizing short-term behavior. Now, taxpayers can get the tax benefit of so-called long-term capital gains if the asset is held for just one year—a period too short to provide a meaningful positive economic impact. While the benefits of the preferential tax treatment for capital gains are ambiguous, there are clear costs of short-term speculation and the myopic short-termism to which it gives rise. There should be a surtax on short-term capital gains given the negative externality of the trading behavior incentivized.

Indeed, in their recent work Patrick Bolton and Frederic Samama propose that corporations themselves provide incentives to long-term investors through "loyalty shares."[20] The firm would require shareholders to hold stock for a set time period before rewarding additional returns. There is no silver bullet here, but by adjusting the rules surrounding corporate governance we can make a significant difference in our economy.

For an additional strategy to improve long-term management of corporations, we suggest that workers must have a say in corporate governance, specifically by including a representative of employees on the corporate board. Further, those managing retirement accounts of any kind should lead the way in acting in the long run interests of the holders of the account. They should be obligated to avoid all conflicts of interest and, especially in the case of worker pensions, ensure the corporations in which they invest act in a responsible way, with good corporate governance and an eye to long-term value, good labor policies, and sound environmental policies.

Rebalance the Tax and Transfer System

Changes to the U.S. tax structure hold enormous potential for reducing inequality and improving the equality of opportunity for Americans—in no small part because the United States ranks among the least redistributive countries in the OECD.[21] Taxes are not only an important way to raise revenue for critical public services and growth-enhancing investments, but they can also improve incentives, encouraging socially desirable economic behavior, and discouraging undesirable behavior, like short-termism. Snowballing changes to the tax code under supply-side rationale over the past 35 years, however, have prioritized tax cuts and subsidies focused on those at the top, placing a greater tax burden on the rest and causing neglect of critical public investments.

We propose an agenda that would use the tax code to structure incentives that reward work, not rent-seeking or speculation. By eliminating the special provisions that distort the economy and increase inequality, we can raise substantial amounts of revenue that can be used for public investments, like education, infrastructure, and technology, that would create a stronger economy, reduce inequalities, and increase opportunity. The most clear-cut changes require raising the top marginal income tax rate, ending preferential treatment of capital gains, cutting the step-up basis at death, and improving enforcement.

Raise the top marginal rate

As we saw in our analysis of the current rules, lower marginal tax rates at the top not only reduce public revenue, but also can distort the economy by actively encouraging rent-seeking. Cuts to the highest marginal tax rate not only increase post-tax and transfer inequality, but also raise the incentive to bargain for more income at the higher end of the income distribution and evade taxes by disguising labor income as capital income.[22] Improving the incentives thus not only raises more revenue, but will improve the equity of pre-tax incomes.

Further, at the highest incomes, many pay much less than they otherwise would due to provisions of the tax code that favor the rich. The current tax policy gives favorable treatment to the forms of income received by the wealthiest Americans. Other taxes like sales and payroll taxes are regressive. Finally, many tax deductions, like the mortgage deduction on second or third homes, favor the rich.

Increasing the marginal tax rate at the top, converting all deductions into tax credits, and limiting the ability to use tax credits would go a long way to restoring progressivity. A 5 percent increase on the top 1 percent's current income tax rate would raise between $1 trillion and $1.5 trillion of additional revenue over 10 years.[23] To put this in perspective: for an extra $50,000 taxed on every $1 million of a wealthy individual's income, the United States could make all public college education free and fund universal pre-K.[24]

Enact a "Fair Tax"

The preferential treatment of capital gains and dividends—income received almost entirely by the richest Americans—is one of the most important reasons that those at the top pay less than ordinary taxpayers. Warren Buffet is famous for pointing out that he pays a lower tax rate than his own secretary. The concentration of capital income is even more extreme than that for labor income. America's wealthiest 0.1 percent pay a *lower* rate than the next wealthiest 0.9 percent.[25] Meanwhile, most Americans earn negligible capital income outside already tax-sheltered retirement savings accounts or on home sales—for which a large exemption exists. Most do not benefit at all from the favorable tax treatment of capital gains, and yet they pay full federal tax rates on their labor income.

A "Fair Tax" is the widely discussed proposal to tax all forms of income at the same rate, which would not only promote fairness but would also reduce the economic inefficiencies caused by the enormous efforts spent by individuals attempting to convert income into forms that are tax-preferred.

We now know that the argument put forward by advocates for capital tax breaks—that they spur investment—is wrong.[26] Rather, cuts in capital gains rates have served to reward speculation as opposed to work. This policy is costly: in 2013 the U.S. government lost $161 billion in revenue as a result of low capital gains tax rates. Further, the CBO estimated that 90 percent of the benefits of this provision went to the wealthiest 20 percent of Americans and 70 percent to the top 1 percent.[27]

The United States should tax capital gains income at the same rate as labor income. To discourage volatile short investments and the associated short-termism that is so widespread today and which undermines long-term investment, short-term capital gains should be taxed at an even higher rate. Targeted tax breaks can be used to incentivize specific forms of productive investment. Because under the current tax regime capital gains are taxed only upon realization—giving owners of capital the opportunity to postpone their taxes—the U.S. should create a "constructive realization" regime, under which capital gains are taxed as they are accrued.

There is one more important change: the provision for step-up in basis at death needs to be eliminated. This provision allows all of the capital gains earned during an individual's life to escape capital gains taxation when the asset is bequeathed, meaning a small number of the wealthiest families pass on wealth free from capital gains tax in perpetuity.

Encourage U.S. investment by taxing corporations on global income

The current U.S. tax code allows corporations to defer paying U.S. taxes on profits earned abroad until the profits are repatriated. The provision has the perverse effect of encouraging corporations to keep profits abroad as opposed to using the funds for U.S. investment. Those who argue the U.S. should tax corporations only on activities that occur within the U.S. are in fact arguing to exacerbate this problem. What many multinationals really want is a race to the bottom: for the U.S. to compete with other countries to get investment by offering the lowest corporate tax possible.

One option is to replace the transfer price system with a formulaic approach that would tax firms on their global income in a fair and comprehensive way, apportioning those profits to the U.S. on the basis of the economic activity—including sales, production, and research—that occurs here. Individual states in the U.S. solved the problem of taxing corporations fairly *among the states* by establishing a formula that assesses the fraction of company sales, employees, and capital within each state, and taxing the firm accordingly.

The U.S. could also establish a complementary minimum tax on all global income—for example, requiring U.S. corporations to pay 10–15 percent on global profits, with a tax credit for taxes paid to other jurisdictions. In doing so, the corporate tax should eliminate differences in marginal effective tax rates between domestic and offshore investment, and be set above a revenue-neutral level. The resulting tax structure would virtually eliminate incentives to move production abroad for tax purposes.

Enact pro-growth, pro-equality tax policies

Beyond the proposals specifically outlined above, there is a range of pro-growth and pro-equality tax reforms that can both raise revenue and rebalance misaligned incentives.[28] One general principle of taxation—known as the Henry George principle—is that we should tax things that have an inelastic supply, like land, oil, or other natural resources. The 19th century progressive Henry George argued that because land does not disappear when taxed, it can be taxed at high levels without negatively distorting the economy; there is effectively no supply response.[29] Even better, we can tax factors or behavior that do harm the economy.

Just as a financial transaction tax would help to curb short-term trading behavior that imposes negative externalities on the broad economy, we should tax pollution (including carbon emissions), a move that can raise revenue while improving economic efficiency.

Eliminating expenditures that distort the economy and accrue to the top is an obvious choice for improving efficiency and reducing inequality. Agriculture subsidies, where most of the money goes to a relatively small number of rich farms or passes through to a relatively small number of monopoly agribusiness processing companies, are one example. But there are many other instances of corporate welfare. Noncompetitive bidding processes for the sale or lease of government-owned natural resources or for the purchase of armaments or prescription drugs under public programs are examples of policies that distort markets and take money away from better uses, even as they enrich those at the top.

GROWING THE MIDDLE

The above recommendations aim to reward productive investment and work, reducing damaging "rents" and maximizing the social benefits of resources and assets. As part of rebalancing, it is equally critical to grow the economy for everyone. We propose four major approaches to spur widespread growth:

- Bring us to full employment, in part by increasing investments in our future.
- Reform the labor market to ensure that everyone benefits from an economy that is working at full steam.
- Reduce the obstacles that exclude working families from accessing opportunities for employment or career growth.
- Provide genuine economic security and opportunity for all Americans by expanding access to the essentials of middle-class life.

We note that this is also an investment agenda. We are investing in our economy, in our workers, and in our people. Whether it's full employment or access to education, these investments are a crucial role that the government must carry out. In that vein, these policies are simultaneously pro-equality and pro-growth. These are ideas that benefit the economy overall, by making people more productive and giving them more opportunities. And they also make sure workers can get their fair share, while ensuring that every American has access to the necessary goods to lead a full and rich life.

Make Full Employment the Goal

Eight years after the Great Recession started, the economy is still not running at full capacity. Labor force participation rates remain significantly below their 2000 levels—in fact, lower than they have been since 1978.[30] There remains a sizable gap between what we could be producing and what we are actually producing. Indeed, we are some 15 percent below where we would have been if the trend growth between 1980 and 2008 had been maintained. A weak labor market, where there is insufficient demand for workers, is one of the reasons that wages have stagnated. More rapid growth accompanied by higher employment would reduce inequality and increase future growth potential. Indeed, with excess capacity and low interest rates—real interest rates at which the government can borrow are actually negative—this is an ideal time to make the investments that would help restore full employment and promote long-term growth.

The federal government can use key macroeconomic tools

to prioritize full employment and tighten labor markets. We propose that the Fed emphasize full employment as the goal of monetary policy and that Congress enact a large infrastructure investment to stimulate growth.

Reform monetary policy to prioritize full employment

In recoveries from recent recessions, the Federal Reserve has raised interest rates prematurely, before labor markets have gained sufficient strength to restore bargaining power to workers. Despite its founding in response to crisis—the Panic of 1907—the Fed has overemphasized low and stable inflation at the expense of full employment and stable output, or even financial stability. This prioritization of price stability is one reason that over the past four decades labor markets have remained slack, wages have grown more slowly than productivity, and workers' share of economic output has declined. As outlined in the previous section, contractionary monetary policy has much stronger unemployment effects for low-wage and often minority workers than for the highest earners.[31]

The Fed should place a greater priority on full employment. In particular, the Fed should resist raising interest rates until wage growth makes up for the lost ground of the Great Recession, even if this means allowing inflation to temporarily overshoot the Fed's 2 percent target. There is no significant risk to the economy from inflation that is far higher than 2 percent.

Rather, there is growing consensus that a higher inflation rate will lead to better economic performance, facilitating adjustments in our highly dynamic and ever-changing economy. The costs of slightly higher inflation are minimal compared to the devastation that comes from prolonged recessions that occur when interest rates remain at or near the zero lower bound.[32]

The Fed must not only rebalance its objectives but also broaden its instruments. It has done this, but only to a limited extent. It used to focus *just* on short-term interest rates. But we now recognize that there are many instruments that affect macroeconomic performance, including economic stability. Had it taken stronger actions against predatory lending, some of the excesses of the pre-crisis period might have been avoided. It should undertake macro-prudential policies to help stabilize the economy. Congress gave it authority to regulate the mortgage market in 1994, and its failure to do so adequately is clearly one of the reasons for the crisis. Regulating margins better might have dampened the tech bubble.

Ensuring that the credit system is actually working and is competitive and not exploitative should be viewed as one of the Fed's responsibilities—and doing so would actually increase the effectiveness of monetary policy. It would make it more likely that a lowering of interest rates would be transmitted to borrowers in the form of lower lending rates—thus stimulating the economy in the way intended. The Fed also has instruments to expand credit availability, which would stimulate the economy even when interest rates are at the zero lower bound.

We should recognize too that putting an excessive burden for macroeconomic stability on monetary policy has been a big mistake. This is especially so in the extreme situation that we have been in since 2007. Monetary policy has been able to stimulate the economy only to a limited extent, and in ways that have actually increased wealth inequality, contributed to a jobless recovery, and increased the risk of future instability. Given the absence of adequate stimulus from fiscal policy, the stance of the Fed is understandable. But we have to be cognizant of the risks.

Reinvigorate public investment

While we have emphasized the importance of rules and regulations and the governance of public institutions like the Federal Reserve in shaping the economy, this is partly because these subjects have been given short shrift. How government spends money also is critical. Among the many benefits of public investment, one is the ability to use fiscal policy along with monetary policy as a lever to achieve full employment. Indeed, as Federal Reserve Chair Janet Yellen noted, "discretionary fiscal policy hasn't been much of a tailwind during this recovery."[33] Further, critical public investments today lay the foundation for long-term economic performance and job growth.

As the country faced competition from abroad, and as advances in technology meant that employment in manufacturing would inevitably go down, we didn't have to face the kind of urban devastation that the country has seen in Baltimore, Gary, and Detroit. Government could have helped in the economic transformation to the new economy—as governments in other countries have done, and as our own government did in other eras. We could have faced up better to the legacy of the inequality of the past, and tried to overcome it with high-quality preschool programs that in other countries have proven to be effective.

We know that public investments in education, technology, and infrastructure are complements to private investment, raising returns and thus "crowding in" such investments. Thus, by making strategic investments, especially in a period when the country faced negative real interest rates, we could have grown the economy, now and in the future, and grown the economy in ways in which there would have been more shared prosperity.

Invest in large-scale infrastructure renovation

America's infrastructure is falling further behind that of other countries.[34] From roads and airports to energy and telecommunication systems, America's failure to even keep up what infrastructure it has makes it more costly to do business and for people to go about their daily lives, and leads to more wasted time and more environmental degradation.[35] Public transit, discussed later in this report, and broadband play a particularly crucial role in connecting all Americans, regardless of income level, with the 21st century local and global job market. Not only are our infrastructure systems crumbling, but they are unequally distributed, leaving distinct areas and communities segregated from the rest of society and without the opportunities that connecting affords.

Our proposal imagines not just restoring America's infrastructure, but a 10-year campaign to make America once again a world leader in job-creating innovation, in part by building a cutting-edge 21st century infrastructure. A comprehensive plan would provide investments in air, rail, and road transportation; public transit; ports and inland waterways; water and energy; and telecommunications and the Internet. Some estimates put the cost of such a project on the order of $4 trillion—well beyond the small sums currently debated but within our means.[36] The investment would yield dividends in the form of more productive businesses, millions of new jobs, and sustainable management of our energy and environmental resources.

Public infrastructure banks have been successful in other countries internationally at financing large infrastructure projects and could prove particularly useful for financing regional projects that cross state lines. The truly costly choice is continuing on the path we are on: doing minimal maintenance to the already deteriorated 20th century infrastructure we now have while other countries upgrade and expand their investments in 21st century infrastructure. Failing to act puts future private investment and employment in the United States at risk; both are at a competitive disadvantage.

Expand access to public transportation

A crumbling public transit system is a clear outgrowth of the decision to use tax policy to reward the richest Americans rather than stimulate investment and growth. Decades of disinvestment in U.S. infrastructure have resulted in high commuting costs that fall disproportionately on low- and middle-income families and decrease access to jobs.

Our existing public transit system is hugely inadequate. Only a little over 50 percent of Americans have any access to public transit at all.[37] Investing in public transit is a matter of equal access to jobs and opportunity, and also a driver of economic performance. If more people can get more access to jobs with which they can live up to their potential, and if they can waste less of their time commuting, then productivity will increase and lives will improve.

According to a Federal Highway Administration report, the total necessary investment in mass transit tops out at $24.5 billion over the next 10 years.[38] This includes the cost of meeting the capital backlog, as well as rehabilitating and expanding transit fleets, facilities, and mass transit rail networks to support projected growth in demand. We should prioritize investment in communities that most require improved access to business centers and job opportunities.

Empower Workers

The goal is not only to create jobs, but also to ensure that workers have a fair say in the workplace. Legal and institutional frameworks have played a far more important role in weakening the wages of American workers than forces such as globalization and technological change. It is within America's power to reinvigorate worker voice and restore balance in the workplace.

Here we propose new rules, designed to strengthen the bargaining power of workers going forward. Our goal is not just a one-time wage increase, but aiding workers in building long-term power to balance the power that corporations have to determine wages, schedules, and employment conditions. We can reinvigorate worker voice, restore balance to the workplace, and give workers a fairer share of the rewards of work and a better chance to contribute to a high-performing workplace.

What follows are policies to expand bargaining power for workers and to set higher standards for all workers through targeted government contracting policies, improved legal enforcement, and a higher minimum wage.

Strengthen the right to bargain

As American citizens, workers by definition possess the right to assemble and petition, yet in many instances, those basic rights have been eviscerated by weaknesses in our national labor policies and legally questionable or downright illegal attacks by employers. Flaws in the National Labor Relations Act place undue burdens and restrictions on workers attempting to organize, while employer aggression is met with inconsistent, insufficient, and untimely penalties.[39] Strategic amendments to the NLRA could protect workers and restore their right to organize.

One flaw in the statute has allowed employers to delay workers' votes to unionize by litigating each step of the process. Recent rule changes issued by the National Labor Relations Board have attempted to rebalance some of the power, and they provide a positive example of how the statutes can be updated to reflect current challenges.

In addition to easing the legal barriers to unionization, stricter penalties are needed to deter illegal intimidation tactics by anti-union employers. Companies seeking to prevent unionization can retaliate by firing workers; if an NLRA violation is found, the employer merely has to reinstate the worker and pay back wages. As if this sanction is not small enough, it is made even more insignificant by the fact that a ruling like this can take more than three years.

Further, the legal framework should be amended to adapt to the changing nature of the workplace. Today, few employers resemble the large manufacturers the creators of the NLRA had in mind. Rather, corporations like Walmart employ a host of personnel through outsourcing and subcontracting, thus bearing little responsibility for the employment relationship. Legal scholars have envisioned new models for defining the employer-employee relationship that would establish clear lines of responsibility within the modern fissured workplace. Specific proposals would redefine the concepts of bargaining unit, employer, secondary action, and the gamut of terms last defined by the federal government in an economy no longer recognizable. Some localities have accomplished this. For example, a case in California established Walmart as the employer of record for employees all along the supply chain and required Walmart to account for wages stolen by subcontractors from subcontracted employees.[40]

Have government set the standards

Laws intended to reverse trends in wages and working conditions are difficult to pass and enforce, but through use of their valuable contracts and licenses, government agencies—especially within more agile city governments—can exert strong influence over private-sector conditions. By attaching strong pro-worker stipulations to their contracts and taxpayer-funded development subsidies, government agencies can raise wages, improve labor standards, and reduce discrimination both within partner entities and in the private sector more broadly.

Following in the footsteps of Los Angeles, federal, state, local, and municipal governments should grant public contracts only to corporations that meet high labor standards and possess strong antidiscrimination/pro-inclusionary hiring practices. Under this practice, contracting agencies would be required to provide a living wage, safe working conditions, and opportunity for advancement, and they would have to submit to regular inspections to ensure compliance. This would not only improve conditions within contracting firms, but—through competition for workers and contracts—across entire industries.[41] President Obama enacted a similar but not as far-reaching example of this policy idea when he raised the minimum wage for federal contractors to $10.10 per hour.

Increase funding for enforcement and raise penalties for violating labor standards

New stories in recent months have highlighted the powerlessness of workers, even in the face of egregious behavior by employers. Low-wage workers face wage theft, improper withholdings, and other violations on a regular basis but often lack the resources to seek recourse. Weak penalties and poor enforcement compound the problem, exposing some of America's most vulnerable workers to even greater insecurity.

Charged with enforcing minimum wage and overtime protections, the Wage and Hour Division of the Department of Labor has seen a third of its inspectors disappear since 1980, despite a doubling of the country's workforce.[42] Since 2009, the agency has managed to recoup $1.1 billion in stolen wages, suggesting both the enormity of the problem and the enormous worker income that could be recovered with proper oversight.[43] Congress should increase the agency's budget to reflect growth of the labor market, the low-wage workforce in particular, and recent evidence of systemic wage theft.

But penalties for minimum wage and overtime infractions are insufficient to deter bad behavior. Given the unlikelihood of workers reporting violations and the lax enforcement when they do, employers can be cavalier about labor law. But overt minimum wage and overtime violation convictions should pose an existential threat to businesses so managers and owners will think twice before engaging in such behavior.

Raise the minimum wage

The minimum wage has been allowed to lose too much of its value. Recent research shows that raising the minimum wage within the range normally discussed has virtually no impact on jobs. Indeed, given the present weakness in aggregate demand, higher incomes might even stimulate the economy. Not only has the government failed to keep the minimum wage near its 1968 value at half the median wage, but family breadwinners have fallen increasingly under the purview of its inadequate protection. An increase in the minimum wage could help reduce working poverty and particularly improve prospects for women, their families, and other disadvantaged groups that are disproportionately represented among minimum wage earners.[44]

We support the proposal to raise the federal minimum wage immediately and to push toward living wages at the state and local level capable of rewarding the dignity of work.* Also, the pitifully lower minimum for tipped workers should be raised to the same floor that applies for all other workers.

Raise the income threshold for mandatory overtime

The New Deal's Fair Labor Standards Act requires that workers who work more than 40 hours a week get overtime pay, at a rate of 150 percent of their regularly hourly wage. However, the act exempts some employers, executives, administrators, and traveling salespeople, among others. To provide a base level of coverage, the Department of Labor has periodically issued a rule that establishes an income threshold under which any employee must be paid for overtime.

The current threshold of $455 a week, or $23,660 a year, was last updated in 2004, and covers just 11 percent of the salaried workforce.[45] In 1975, 65 percent of salaried workers were covered by overtime rules; if the 1975 threshold had kept pace with inflation, 47 percent of workers in 2013, rather than just 11 percent, would have received overtime.[46] To restore this pillar of middle-class income, the Department of Labor should raise

---

* A recent proposal from the Economic Policy Institute calls for a $12.00 federal minimum wage by 2020.

the threshold to ensure that once again the majority of salaried workers are covered.

Expand Access to Labor Markets and Opportunities for Advancement

The challenges faced by women and people of color in the workforce go well beyond individual racism or implicit bias. Indeed, structural racism enforced through an uncountable network of rules and policies including poor public investment in minority communities, aggressive policing, and historical exclusion prevents people of color from accessing opportunities for work and economic success. A similar web of power and rules prevents women from achieving full equality in the workforce.

We require an agenda that creates opportunity to succeed and advance for the 21st century workforce, a workforce that predominantly consists of women and people of color. Here we propose just a few priority policies that will go some distance toward rooting out labor force discrimination and improve prospects for America's workers. We must dismantle legal structures that explicitly prevent people of color from equally competing in the workforce, including an egregious system of incarceration and a broken immigration system. In addition, we must expand the structures that support working women and families overall.

Tackling these barriers to employment will increase opportunity for millions and expand overall productivity.

Reform the criminal justice system to reduce incarceration rates

The United States incarcerates a higher percentage of its population than any other nation in the world at a huge cost to individuals and families as well as to economic performance. The overall societal and human impacts of mass incarceration, in terms of effects on children, families, and particularly people of color, warrant and have received their own political agenda and movement. Much of that work is beyond the scope of this report. Here we focus specifically on the clear economic consequences of incarcerating 2.3 million people, more than 1 percent of all adults in the United States (and 2.3 percent of all African-Americans).[47] We recommend specific reforms to expunge the records, reduce mandatory minimum sentences, improve legal representation, and curtail unjust levies.

In addition to the high price of running the world's largest prison system, mass incarceration reduces employment opportunities and wages, and increases dependency on public assistance for a large share of the population. A study by the Vera Institute for Justice found that the total public cost of incarceration was more than $31,000 per inmate in 2010. Incarceration is costly, too, for those who have been locked up and end up facing lower hourly wages, annual employment, and annual earnings. That burden falls disproportionately on men of color.[48]

One key driver of underemployment is the employment penalty for felons. One study estimates that prison records and felony convictions reduced the overall male unemployment rate by 1.5–1.7 percentage points in 2008 alone.[49] Congress should move to reduce the burden ex-felons face when searching for jobs by expunging certain records after a set amount of time.

Further, mandatory minimum sentencing particularly targets people of color. A U.S. Sentencing Commission report to Congress found that African-Americans and Latinos accounted for 69.8 percent of mandatory minimum sentences in 2010;[50] tackling this issue will effectively reduce part of the inequality inherent in the nation's sentencing rules. Congress also should immediately allow judges the ability to waive mandatory minimums. The Department of Justice should focus on encouraging alternatives to incarceration, investigating possible best practices that can be adopted at the federal and state levels.

The inaccessibility of quality legal representation results in disproportionately harsh sentencing for the poorest. According to a report from the Brennan Center of Justice, a concerted effort to reclassify nonjailable offenses, increase public defense funding, and improve effectiveness through regular attorney and social worker training would ensure more equitable access to representation.[51]

Similarly, onerous fees at every level of the criminal justice system generate severe financial burdens for the poor and create further points of entry back into the incarceration system. A society-wide effort is needed here, including debt collection efforts targeted at ability to pay, eliminating public defender fees, and eliminating escalation of fees for those who cannot pay the first time.

Reform immigration law by providing a pathway to citizenship

Estimates indicate more than 11 million undocumented immigrants live and work in the shadows of the U.S. economy, in every corner of the country and every sector of work.[52] Self-deportation and mass deportation clearly are not credible solutions, nor are they desirable. Not only does America's broken immigration system inhumanely tear families apart, it is also costly to businesses facing risks of an uncertain labor supply and communities where exploitation of undocumented immigrants drives down wages and working conditions throughout the labor market. Employment practices targeting those demanding decent treatment and payment of back wages have resulted in retaliatory actions against U.S. citizens and immigrant workers alike, but undocumented immigrants have no recourse and the threat of raids from U.S. Immigration and Customs Enforcement is a heavy damper on worker complaints about working conditions and wage theft.[53]

To bring these people out of the shadows and fully vest their contributions from working, starting businesses, and paying taxes in the United States, the federal government must provide a pathway to citizenship for those already here and simplify the process by which new migrants can continue to come and contribute to America's economic success. Nothing short of this path will solve the problem of exploitation of immigrant workers, but there are steps to take now to improve the situation of those undocumented immigrants already here and integrated into our economy and society.

The first step is to cease the deportation and internment of all but violent criminals and to normalize the legal status of families working, learning, and serving in America.

The second is to better coordinate the efforts of different parts of government to enforce immigration laws in ways that don't undermine the conditions for people working here. This means that U.S. Immigration and Customs Enforcement, or ICE, should take a back seat to the Department of Labor to ensure that unscrupulous employers cannot easily threaten workers with the prospect of deportation by calling in worksite raids.[54] Third, Congress should act to ensure that all labor laws extend to all people working in America, irrespective of their documentation status. No one who works an honest day in America should be afforded fewer protections at work just because they don't have a piece of paper.

Legislate paid sick leave

Today nearly 40 percent of the workforce doesn't have access to paid sick days. For at least 43 million private-sector workers, taking a day off to care for themselves or for loved ones means risking their job. States and localities across the country have been implementing paid sick leave policies. In Connecticut, the first state to pass paid sick leave, a recent survey of employers found that three-quarters now support the policy; a survey in San Francisco found two-thirds in support, and one in Seattle came in at 70 percent.[55] Federal legislation should aim toward universal coverage.

Legislate paid family leave

The United States is one of the only countries in the world without nationwide legislation in place to support paid parental leave for new parents. Many OECD countries guarantee up to 52 weeks of paid parental leave, with guarantees in place for both mothers and fathers.[56] The U.S. failure to provide paid parental leave continues to limit economic opportunities for women in particular, but makes it more difficult for both men and women to take time off to care for their children.

Plenty of evidence documents the benefits of these human capital investment policies for child development.[57] Further, reducing the penalty for working women who give birth could increase the female labor force participation rate, which in turn would boost U.S. productivity.[58] An OECD study suggests that just 15 weeks of paid maternity leave would have a measurable impact on productivity growth.[59] In addition, normalizing paternity leave not only increases men's participation in family life but also begins to transform the workplace.

The United States should craft federal family leave policies like the ones that have been successful internationally. First, family leave should be universally available to workers. Second, parents of both sexes should be covered. To truly achieve equity in the workplace and in the home, men and women must be offered the same protections for care-giving. Third, family leave policies must include job protection for pregnant workers.

One effective model would create an independent trust fund within the Social Security Administration to collect fees and provide benefits to employees. The benefits would be available to every individual regardless of employer size or employment type, and would allow workers to take paid leave for their own health concerns, including pregnancy and childbirth recovery; birth and adoption; the serious health condition of children, parents, spouses, or domestic partners; and military caregiving and leave purposes.[60]

Subsidize childcare

Just as U.S. family leave lags other advanced nations, U.S. provisions for childcare lag those of other advanced countries. Expanding access and quality would benefit children and increase women's workforce participation.

A robust and effective childcare regime would provide a menu of supports to families all along the income spectrum, from birth to kindergarten. For lower-income families, early childhood learning, whether it's home visiting or Head Start, helps close the achievement gap for children and improve maternal earnings. For middle-class families, broad access to childcare would help boost women's workforce participation and provide much-needed relief for families that face high childcare costs without the benefits of government subsidies.

With the long-term goal of providing affordable childcare to all American families, Congress should start by expanding the most effective existing state and federal programs. Scaling up the current childcare policies and programs would give parents needed supports in raising their children, and would also allow them to get and hang on to jobs, benefitting their families and the economy more broadly.

Promote pay equity

Despite passage of the Equal Pay Act half a century ago, women continue to earn less than men across occupations. As we note earlier, as of 2014, women earned slightly more than 82 cents in weekly wages for every dollar earned by a man. The burden of unequal pay falls doubly hard on women of color. While white women earn an average of 78 percent of what white men earn, African-American and Latina women earn an average of just 64 percent and 56 percent of white male wages.[61]

The structural obstacles to closing the wage gap are manifold and include those listed above: access to childcare and family leave, along with a host of other dynamics. One clear obstacle to wage equity, however, is that almost half of all U.S. workers are either strongly discouraged or under contract not to share their salaries with colleagues.

Protect women's access to reproductive health services

Without the ability to make informed decisions about their health and access affordable quality care when they need it, plan the timing and size of their families, and have healthy pregnancies and births, women will never be able to take full advantage of the economic opportunities available to them. For example, the only federal program dedicated to providing affordable family planning services has been underfunded for decades. The return on investment is extraordinary: in 2010 every dollar invested in Title X family planning programs, first instituted under the 1970 Public Health Service Act, saved $7.09 in taxpayer dollars.[62] We should ensure that all women can access needed family planning and reproductive health services.

Expand Economic Security and Opportunity

Much of the insecurity felt by Americans today stems from the fact that the essentials to a middle-class life are increasingly out of reach. The price of a good life—one that allows a family to educate its children, provide a stable home, save something in case of emergency, and retire at a reasonable age—is more than most can afford.

We propose an agenda to ease the financial strain for America's families. We seek to expand access to early education and higher education. By bringing down the costs of health care, we aim to help families avoid financial catastrophe. We call for reforms to ensure Americans have reliable access to finance, as well as an expansion to Social Security. Finally, we propose voting reforms to ensure more Americans have a say in our democratic system.

Invest in early childhood through child benefits, home visiting, and pre-K

Investments in early childhood learning are among the most critical for human development and the most effective in terms of productivity. A true investment agenda would prioritize funding for evidence-based programs that provide children from birth to age 5 with the opportunity to succeed in life.

A priority should be investing in those most at risk: the 22 percent of U.S. children living in poverty, including 39 percent of African-American children and 32 percent of Latino children.[63] Recent research has confirmed what most already know: childhood poverty has debilitating lifelong effects, but interventions are capable of breaking the cycle of intergenerational poverty. As our society grows richer, it is essential we make the long-term investments in children.

Programs focused on child health and education are critical long-term investments. Countless evidence-based randomized control trials have shown the state run Maternal, Infant, and Early Childhood Home Visiting Program to be one of the most effective investments of taxpayer dollars.[64] By supporting new mothers in good parenting habits like speaking frequently to their babies or breast-feeding long-term, home visiting programs help reduce the growing gap in outcomes between children born into poor homes and rich homes. Research on high-quality programs shows improved impacts for participating mothers, who are more likely than their counterparts to rejoin the workforce; reduced needs for government assistance; and improved life outcomes.[65] The children also have improved school readiness.[66]

One proposal that should be considered is a universal child benefit, a monthly tax-free stipend paid to families with children under 18 to help offset part of the cost of raising kids. In this we can follow several peer nations that have successfully reduced child poverty to a large degree through such programs. The U.K., for instance, recently cut its child poverty by more than half through a package of anti-poverty measures, including a universal child benefit.[67]

Children from families at all income levels would benefit from an expansion of the kinds of quality universal preschool programs already implemented in a number of states and localities through a variety of providers and funding mechanisms. At the federal level, Congress could immediately expand funding to provide pre-K childcare subsidies to all currently eligible children. This would expand access to 12 million children at a cost of $66.5 billion.[68]

Increase access to higher education through more public financing, restructuring student loans, and increasing scrutiny of for-profit schools

Higher education is one of the building blocks of our economy. However, reduced public support, plus the increasing presence of inadequately regulated for-profit institutions willing and able to exploit some of America's disadvantaged, has undermined our ability to educate the workforce. We propose increasing public funding for higher education, restructuring student lending by providing income-based repayment plans and reforming bankruptcy laws, and bringing for-profit schools under greater scrutiny.

Even when emerging from World War II and saddled with a debt ratio larger than Greece's in 2010, the U.S. committed itself to providing a free education to returning soldiers.[69] The G.I. Bill helped create the middle-class society that we had aspired to—the first such society in the world. Yet, some say that today, though we are so much richer, we can't afford even more modest programs. This is wrong. We should realize that we cannot afford not to ensure that all young Americans get the best education for which they are qualified so they can live up to their potential.

For too long, we've been trying to increase educational access through tax credits for middle-class families and grants for the poor. This approach has not achieved the desired results. We should build on the president's recent free community college plan but go well beyond it. We should recognize that our major research universities educate our young people and produce research that fuels innovations that drive business and change the way we live. These are natural complementary goods, and joining these two activities together is one of the reasons for the world-leading excellence of our university system. But research is a national public good (or indeed a global public good) and should be nationally funded. And with the increased mobility of educated people, even ensuring that we have a talented pool of highly skilled workers has become a national public good. Our education policy should reflect these changes.

Meanwhile, $1 trillion is outstanding in student loans.[70] It is already having an impact in reduced life prospects, from having to forgo work at jobs dedicated to the public good simply because they don't pay enough, to forcing our young people to postpone building families. Going forward, the government should look to follow the lead of Australia and adopt universal income-based repayment, in which repayment consists of a set percentage of future income. Students could then repay their student debts more easily—at much lower transactions costs— through withholding.

An important step here is to restore the protections available to those with student loans. Studies have shown that removing bankruptcy protection for those with student loans, particularly in the 2005 policy change under the Bankruptcy Abuse Prevention and Consumer Protection Act, has done nothing to reduce bankruptcy filings resulting in costly defaults.[71] It has, however, increased stress enormously, and extracted money from poor students that goes into the coffers of the banks. The government should restore those protections.

Affordability is not the only concern. We must ensure that students are receiving the kind of high-quality education that will prepare them to be engaged citizens in the 21st century. One immediate way to improve outcomes for graduates is to increase scrutiny of for-profit schools, which receive a large share of government-funded loans or government-guaranteed loans while often failing to provide students with a quality education. Eighty-seven percent of revenues at for-profits come from federal or state sources, including student loans and Pell grants. Though they teach around 10 percent of students, they account for about 25 percent of total Department of Education student aid program funds. Studies show that those at for-profit schools do poorly compared to those at community colleges. Completion rates are poor, as is success in getting a job.[72] Under the current administration, the Department of Education has reviewed outcomes for graduates from for-profit institutions and found them lacking. Proposed regulations would establish a set of requirements for all institutions receiving federally funded or backed loans—a strong step in the right direction.[73]

Make health care affordable and universal

Market forces have not worked well at controlling costs in our health care system and delivering broadly available quality care. The health care system is rife with the kinds of market failures that economists have studied extensively, including information asymmetries and imperfections in competition.

Hospitals, physician networks, and health care insurers increasingly operate in conditions approaching monopolies.[74] Patients largely have neither the medical expertise to perform the cost-benefit analyses necessary for making optimizing choices about the care they need, nor the access to price information for comparison shopping, leaving providers to determine both the demand and supply of health care. The result of our market-driven health care system is that people in the United States pay higher prices for virtually every aspect of health care than those in other advanced economies, and even with the big steps forward in the Affordable Care Act, 12 percent of Americans are still left without health coverage.[75] In spite of our high expenditures, health outcomes are poorer.

We propose building on health care system changes already underway to control overall health care spending in the United States, while increasing the quality of care and reducing overall inequality.

Medicare, with its superior record of controlling health care costs and delivering higher-quality outcomes than private insurers, is an exceptionally popular and successful public policy. And Medicare achieves these outcomes while insuring the highest-risk and most expensive patients: senior citizens.

Opening Medicare to all would yield three significant improvements in addition to providing more people access to a high-quality, low-cost health insurance plan. First, competition from Medicare's entry into the insurance exchange would lower premiums for everyone; one study found increased competition on exchanges could lower fees by an estimated 11 percent.[76] Second, Medicare's wider acceptance by providers than many private insurers would provide an alternative to the lower-premium "skinny network" plans offered that limit choices to a highly restricted set of doctors and hospitals in many markets. Third, introducing Medicare as viable competition will also drive employer-provided health plans purchased from ACA exchanges toward the higher efficiency and standards offered by Medicare.

Making Medicare open to all would, of course, require several adjustments to the program, including integrating its doctor, hospital, and prescription coverage and adding coverage for providers serving needs beyond the population of senior citizens.

Expand access to banking services through a postal savings bank

Nearly 93 million Americans—about 28 percent—are unbanked or underbanked, and that number is unlikely to budge.[77] Having access to the payment system is a necessary condition of living and working in the modern economy, and far too many people can only access it on the most predatory terms. They simply don't know whether hidden somewhere in the complicated contracts will be terms to their detriment. These worries are well-justified, given the rash of abusive practices exposed in the aftermath of the financial crisis.

The Postal Service should be authorized to create a "post card" debit card available with minimum fees and high protections for consumers. Its scale and size would significantly allow both access and efficiency to help citizens build wealth, and it would force banks and payday lenders to actually compete on price and services rather than confusion and predation. The overwhelming success of the Direct Express card for receiving Social Security and other benefits through electronic payments can serve as a model.

Merchants too would benefit, as the new card would charge just enough to cover costs—not enough to generate the tens of billions of dollars made by the credit and debit card companies. And the lower costs faced by merchants would be passed on to ordinary consumers through lower prices. So, while this is a reform that seems targeted at America's unbanked, there would be trickle-up benefits throughout the entire economy.

Create a public option for housing finance

The housing finance market remains broken seven years after the financial crisis. While private securitization (other than through Fannie Mae and Freddie Mac) provided over 50 percent of the mortgage-backed securities in 2006, since the crisis that number has been less than 5 percent.[78] It shows no sign of changing; public-sector institutions still underwrite the vast majority of all conventional mortgages. Private market securitization remains flat, accounting for a very small fraction of total housing financing. Efforts to create a public-private hybrid system in Congress have stalled, given reasonable concerns about future bailouts and the inability to properly regulate such a system. And America's banks have resisted demands that if they originate mortgages, they should have "skin in the game," i.e., bear the consequences for the bad mortgages they originate. The suits that emerged after the financial crisis exposed fraud, incompetence, and negligence beyond the imagination of even the sector's critics. Wall Street has been unable to police itself, with no systematic reforms coming from the industry itself to try and rebuild its mortgage system.

Many in the private sector want to resurrect a version of the old system that worked so well for them, with government guarantees backstopping their lending practices. Rather than trying to nudge the private mortgage system with federal backstops, subsidies, and implicit bailout guarantees, lawmakers should create an explicitly public mechanism in the housing market. While the private sector excelled in exploiting ordinary Americans, it fell short in designing financial products that would help ordinary Americans manage the risks associated with home ownership. A broken housing finance system keeps people from building assets by making the most significant investment of their life, exposes people to higher costs of rental housing, and forces them to forgo the social capital built when people invest in building a home, not just a house.

The key information needed for issuing good mortgages already lies in the public domain of IRS records and property registries: an individual's income history and the prices of similar houses. We know too that new technologies mean that in the 21st century, the cost of processing this information should have become negligible.

All of this points to the creation of a 21st century housing finance system—including a government homeownership agency—using modern technology and the lessons learned from around the world on financial products that are best suited to the management of risk for ordinary individuals. This would lead to low transactions costs and efficient risk products—so different from what has been happening in the U.S., where the financial sector has looked for products that maximize fees (transactions costs) and that fine tune the ability to exploit different groups. This new arrangement should be able not only to deliver better financial products, but lower costs to just a little more than the interest rates the government pays on the money it borrows.

This new entity would supply housing loans in ways that provide explicit benefits to borrowers—a far better way of supporting ordinary Americans than the trickle-down approach based on supplying government subsidies to private developers. Properly structured, this public option can easily provide the 21st century mortgage financing system that our struggling economy—and America's struggling families—need. And it would provide the kind of competition that might incentivize the private financial sector to better perform the functions that it is supposed to perform.

Increase retirement security by reducing transactions costs and the exploitation of retirees, and expanding Social Security

Our system of private retirement savings remains weak and inefficient. The fact that more people in America will face retirement with inadequate savings poses problems not just for the retirees, but for the overall economy as their consumption will contract with inadequate retirement income, or they will divert consumption from others in their families or rely more heavily on social transfers.

We need to strengthen our retirement system by reducing transactions costs and the exploitation of retirees. Expanding the Social Security system to include a "public option" for additional annuity benefits would enhance competition, driving down costs and increasing services.

The transfer of retirement accounts from large pension pools to individual accounts has increased overall administration fees. Research shows that the average 401(k) participant could lose up to a third of future savings in fees.[79] Meanwhile, asset management fees have been a top driver of Wall Street's revenues in the last two decades.[80] A simple change in the rules, requiring fund managers to adhere to a fiduciary standard, would be an important move in the right direction.

But, again, we could do more. We could require, for instance, that any pension or retirement account eligible for preferential tax treatment not have excessive transactions costs. Fees on any account could not exceed those on the best-performing indexed funds, unless there were demonstrably higher risk-adjusted returns. (Any excess fees would be held in an escrow account until the higher performance over, for example, a 10-year period were demonstrated.) This reform would simultaneously reduce the exploitation of savers that results in significant reductions in their retirement income, reduce inequality, and reduce the short-termism prevalent in the economy.

Our system of public retirement savings, in the form of Social Security, remains strong and effective. Administrative costs are but a fraction of those in the private sector, and recipients of Social Security are protected against fluctuations in stock prices and inflation. The main concern with our public Social Security program is budgetary: there is a worry that it is not self-sustaining. Whether it is or is not depends on a large number of variables that will inevitably change over the relevant time horizon—the next half-century. What is clear is that we may need to make adjustments as time goes on. And there are many ways that we can make such adjustments.

For example, we should remove the payroll cap that limits the amount of revenue Social Security raises. In addition, the government should expand retirement security by providing a voluntary public retirement program above Social Security to further supplement retirement security. The plan could be modeled on private individual retirement accounts (IRA), but the public program would have many additional benefits. Lower transaction costs and reduced opportunities for exploitation are immediate advantages. But the government could also match savings for the worse off—the opposite of our current system for encouraging savings, which overwhelmingly subsidizes the rich.* Such a program, what might be thought of as a public option for retirement, would be unsubsidized, but would provide competition and standards for the private sector. In the end, all would benefit from this greater *true* competition in financial services.

Reform political inequality

Enacting the bold reforms we outline in this report, as well as other measures to address wealth and income inequality, is as much about political will as it is about economics. The concentration of wealth in our economy has created a concentration of power in our democracy. The result is that policies favored by the wealthy receive attention, while policy preferences of poor and middle-income Americans are ignored.[81]

Today, we have inequality in our democracy: people with

---

* This can be partially paid for by capping the deductibility of 401(k) savings among the rich.

higher incomes vote more frequently than those with lower incomes and election campaign finance is dominated by a relatively small number of large donors who wield outsize influence.[82] While there are a number of reforms needed to build a more inclusive democracy, two in particular stand out as having the most potential to create equality of voice in our democracy.

The first is making voting easy. Our current system of voting discourages full participation, leaving rules to the states, many of which have erected unnecessary barriers such as burdensome voter registration practices, in-person voting, voting on a weekday, long wait times, and onerous voter identification. We should establish a federal system of universal voting that includes: (1) automatic voter registration, accepted throughout the country without the need to reregister and without burdensome voter identification requirements; (2) the ability to vote by mail or early in-person on multiple days; (3) the establishment of weekend Election Days or a national election holiday; and (4) online voting when cyber-security concerns are met.

Second, it is critical that we create a campaign finance system less dominated by large contributions. A constitutional amendment could go a long way toward allowing Congress greater leeway to reform campaign finance laws to increase political equality. Yet even within today's legal framework, it is both possible and imperative to enact a system of public funding to match small-donor political contributions. Under this system, candidates can raise enough money to compete for elected office by raising small-dollar contributions and relying much less on wealthy donors.

There are still other reforms, like requiring shareholders to vote in support of any political contributions. This report has emphasized the *economic* reforms that are needed to restore the American *economic* dream. But our democratic ideals too are an important part of the American dream. Inequalities created by the rules and institutions that govern our political process need to change, too.

CONCLUSION

Our economy is a large and complex system and, in order to solve the problems with that system, we must aim to fix the economy as a whole. The financial crisis of 2008 and the Great Recession that followed exposed the inadequacy of the old economic models; the new research and thinking that has emerged as a result suggests that equality and economic performance are in fact complementary rather than opposing forces. No more false choices: changing course won't be easy in the current environment, but we can choose to fix the rules structuring our system. By doing so, we can restore the balance between government, business, and labor to create an economy that works for everyone. Building on the innovative legacy of the New Deal, we must tame the growth of wealth among the top 1 percent and establish rules and institutions that ensure security and opportunity for the middle class.

APPENDIX

Overview of recent inequality trends

Most Americans remain preoccupied with the increasingly difficult task of managing their own household economic situation, rather than worrying about how a small sliver of the population managed to amass such extreme fortunes over the past several decades. This report advances the view that these two trends are inextricably linked—both the result of changes in the rules, laws, and policies that structure how our economy functions.

The American economy no longer works for most people in the United States. We know this from a raft of economic data showing the trends: a small percentage of the population takes home the lion's share of economic gains while most of the population faces stagnant wages and increasing financial stress as they attempt to secure the traditional staples of a middle-class life.

But in fact, the rise of inequality in the United States is still much worse than most realize—in economics, politics, or the general public—or the most often cited statistics indicate. Not only has inequality risen to alarming levels unparalleled in other advanced economy countries, but the American dream of the prospects for individual economic advancement also increasingly appears to be a myth: high levels of inequality and wealth are associated with low levels of opportunity for upward economic mobility. More people are working hard, but not getting ahead—a fact we see across a range of indicators beyond the standard view of stagnant wages.

Hourly wages for most workers increased a mere 0.1 percent per year on average since 1980 after adjusting for inflation; between 2000 and 2013 the median family income actually *decreased* by 7 percent.[1]

Although the federal poverty line provides an imperfect measure of basic needs, an estimated 2.8 million people worked full-time year round and still fell below the poverty line.[2] Inadequate incomes are not due to a lack of effort—compared to 1979 the average middle class family worked an additional 14 full-time weeks per year in 2007, before the Great Recession impacted employment levels.[3]

These income pressures are worse for some people at certain times of life. Families needing childcare, attempting to send a child to college, or facing a health emergency have few additional funds and sharply rising costs—and so are under acute financial stress. And problems of adequate incomes pose disproportionate problems to women and people of color who have yet to shake the structural exclusion from certain occupations and discrimination in pay relative to men and whites in the workplace.

Wages and incomes for the majority of U.S. workers are no longer connected to how productive they are on the job. Conventional economic theory suggests that, in an efficient economy, workers should be paid based upon what they contribute to production.* However, what workers are paid has, for the past generation, lagged far beyond their productivity. Historically these two indicators grew in tandem, but in the 40 years between 1973 and 2013, the relationship between worker output per hour, or labor productivity, and compensation began to break down. Labor productivity, or average output per hour of work, increased 161 percent while compensation paid to workers—including wages and other non-wage benefits—rose only 19 percent after adjusting for inflation.[4] (While employers paid slightly more in total compensation, this largely reflected an increase in costs of health care benefits paid by employers. In other words workers didn't see any increase in their standards of living.)

In addition to low wages, getting a decent job remains a

---

* Economic theory says that wages should move with marginal productivity, but historically, average and marginal productivity have moved together, so much so that a standard model used by macroeconomists assumes that the two are proportional. There is no evidence that a significant wedge has opened up in movements in marginal and average productivities. Hence, we must look elsewhere for an explanation of relative wage stagnation.

challenge for many Americans. Even as the national unemployment rate fell to 5.4 percent as of April 2015, most American families know the labor market remains weak.[5] The overall share of the U.S. population at work—a broader measure of labor market activity than the unemployment rate—remains at around 59 percent. This is well below pre-recession levels and far below the peak of the nearly 65 percent employment-to-population ratio reached at the tail end of the 1990s economic boom.[6] Even among those counted as employed, 6.7 million people are working part time because they can't find full-time work, a 54 percent increase from 10 years ago.[7]

These declining prospects for work are a direct result of the structural factors discussed at length in the section of this report entitled "The Current Rules." For example, the Federal Reserve has chosen to prioritize price stability over full-employment, and thus failed to keep labor markets tight. The federal government has used fiscal (tax) policy to reward high-income earners rather than to make critical public investments that boost growth and compensation. Regulatory and legal changes have incentivized the private sector to prioritize short-term gains rather than the long-term investments in capital, research, or training that increase productivity. Additionally, we have seen a comprehensive campaign attacking existing labor standards and obstructing efforts adopt new ones. Finally, our legal and institutional structures have made remarkably little progress in reducing the obstacles to good jobs faced by women and people of color.

FALLING LABOR SHARE OF INCOME MOST PRONOUNCED IN BOTTOM 99 PERCENT

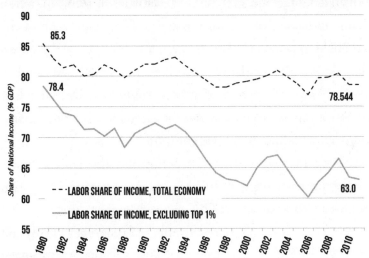

FIGURE A1

Source: Giovannoni, Olivier. 2014. "What Do We Know About the Labor Share and the Profit Share? Part III: Measures and Structural Factors." Levy Economics Institute working paper no. 805, cross posted as UTIP working paper no. 66.

If the income gains from more productive work did not go to U.S. workers, where did they go? The answer can be seen in Figure A1, which shows income from labor as a share of total income in the United States from 1980 to 2011. The dashed line indicates that the share of income paid to labor fell to 78.5 percent in 2011 from 85.3 percent as investors and wealth holders took a commensurately larger share of national income. But capital income is not the only thing to increase for the economically best-off during this time. The labor income—meaning salaries—of the top 1 percent (largely corporate executives and financial sector professionals) skyrocketed as well. Lumped in with all labor income, even national statistics showing an overall decline in labor share of income give a false impression of the share paid to workers.[8] Disaggregating helps us see the problem more closely. Economist Olivier Giovannoni analyzed the data to see what the labor share of income would look like, excluding income of the top 1 percent, and showing a much more precipitous decline: falling to 63 percent from 78.5 percent.[9]

Rising inequality over this period put the United States among the most unequal of high income countries: only two countries within the OECD showed higher levels market income inequality, and, once the effect of progressive taxes and public transfer payments are taken into account, no advanced country is more unequal than the United States.[10] The United States is much less generous in redistributing income than other countries, which is even starker when researchers focus solely on working-age populations under 60, as most people retire at a younger age outside the United States.[11]

A political focus on the fact that top incomes have risen enormously while the majority of the population faces economic stress does not imply envy—the trends at the top are inextricably linked to the trends across the rest of the income distribution. Rising inequality undermines the opportunity for upward economic mobility. Research across OECD countries shows that the United States ranked poorly among advanced economy countries on the extent of its economic mobility.[12] Reports from the Economic Policy Institute and the Urban Institute illustrate just how immobile the United States is. These studies explored the likelihood that a person starting out in either the top or bottom quintile in 1994 would move to a different income quintile by 2004. More than 93 percent of people starting out at the bottom did not rise to more than the middle-income group over 10 years. In comparison, 80 percent of those starting in the top income group remained in the top or second to top after 10 years.[13]

Beyond affecting the functioning of our economy, the way that rising inequality at the top restrains economic mobility concerns the nature of our society and democracy. Economists now know that there is a strong association between the level of inequality in society and the degree of economic mobility.[14] This is true not only when we look across countries, but even across regions in the U.S. Not surprisingly, the greater inequality experienced in the U.S. since 1980 seems to have decreased opportunity. What little progress the United States had experienced with improving income mobility has stopped and the country has become more socially rigid. Economist Nathaniel Hilger found sizable improvements in intergenerational mobility in cohorts born between 1940 and 1980—a period of significant gains for social justice, including the expansion of education and important civil rights victories. This is also the period that saw the strongest declines in inequality.[15] Since then, the rate of upward mobility has flattened: the probability of moving out of the income group one is born into is astonishingly low and not improving.[16] As inequality grows, the consequences of stalled intergenerational mobility become more severe. Using the familiar ladder analogy, we observe that, even if the chances of climbing remain constant, the growing distance between rungs greatly increases the difficulty of the climb, amplifying the value of the "birth lottery."[17]

There are two reasons to worry: First, given recent increases in inequality of income, it would be a surprise if inequality of opportunity did not worsen in the future. Second, to get ahead in a modern economy, one needs a good education. But the quality of education one receives is closely tied to the socioeconomic status and education of parents (particularly fathers).[18]

Evidence of inequality by economic status, race, and gender pervade our education and health systems.[19] But the development that occurs during the early stage of life is much more unequal and has lifelong consequences for an individual's cognitive development and economic success. Where a family sits on the income and wealth scales affects how much they have access to and can benefit from human capital expenditures and investments—from the quality of prenatal and maternal care, to the quality of childcare and the early development environment, to whether the parent's job affords family and sick leave.

Inequality at the starting gate begins long before a child reaches formal education systems. And it follows children, compounding throughout their academic and professional careers.[20] The quality of one's early environment matters tremendously. Nobel laureate James Heckman studied extensively how intensive pre-education pilot programs affect low-income children through schooling and into adulthood.[21] Heckman found that children receiving access to these programs performed better in school, were more likely to graduate and go to college, and were less likely to smoke, use drugs, become teenage mothers, or go on welfare.

An overwhelming body of research in this area shows that quality early childcare is the most consistent predictor of a young child's behavioral and developmental outcomes including language, interpersonal communication, and cognitive abilities.[22] Already, by the time children enter kindergarten, studies find significant impacts of early learning and environment. In one study, kindergarteners from low-income families exhibited weaker academic and attention skills.[23] Children contending with hunger and inadequate nutrition also show impaired learning in school.[24]

Unequal access to affordable, quality childcare and early learning opportunities are compounded by the increasing time strains placed on working parents.[25] The secular trend over the past generation toward greater labor force participation by women and longer hours worked by everyone, especially single parents, leave little time or material resources left to invest in children's human capital development. The problem is further compounded for people residing in segregated areas, which are traditionally underserved by public transportation and other services. People in segregated areas also disproportionately have precarious, uncertain schedules and must also spend long hours commuting and running errands instead of, for example, helping their children with their homework.[26]

Unlike early childhood and postsecondary education that families must pay for, kindergarten-through-12th grade education is ostensibly free in the United States. But of course educational quality and resources vary tremendously depending on locale—and competition to live in high-quality school districts prices many out of the market.[27]

Although America has long canonized the rags-to-riches narrative, the likelihood of that story becoming a reality has greatly decreased. As inequality rises, the political system becomes increasingly over-run by corporate interests, and the public policies required to provide real equality of opportunity become harder and harder to enact.

The Role of Technology and Globalization

Many experts now agree that inequality is a significant challenge that must be addressed, but disagree on the causes and commensurate solutions to tackling the problems. Traditional arguments focus on technology or globalization as inequality's root causes. But the United States is not different from others who also face increasing computerization and automation in the workplace, as well as increasing competition from international trade and investment. But we do stand out in the excesses of our inequality.

This report focuses on the rules of our economy and the multiple policies that determine how it functions. But to understand why we focus on those structural policy elements, it is important to discuss other explanations for the particular type inequality we are seeing today in the U.S. Many experts agree that inequality is a significant challenge that must be addressed. But, following traditional economic arguments, they argue that rising inequality has little to do with the rules of the economy and much more to do with the rise of globalization and increasingly sophisticated technology. These stories are either unconvincing, in the case of technology, or insufficient, in the case of globalization.

There are three reasons to find the technology and globalization stories, as explanations for job loss and wage slowdown, at best only part of the story. First, as we have already mentioned, other countries around the world face the same global changes with respect to technology and international trade, yet have experienced nowhere near the rise of inequality seen in the United States. Many of these other countries have managed to shape their economies in ways that have produced more shared prosperity, with equivalent economic growth performance. With common exposure to technology and globalization, logic dictates some other variables must be the cause of America's uniquely extreme level of inequality.

Second, these technology and globalization stories are really primarily about supply and demand for labor as the sole determinant of wages. They seek to interpret changes in inequality simply as the outcome of shifts in demand and supply curves, explained in turn by changes in technology and globalization. But institutions matter as well. One of the important advances in economic theory over the past several decades, for which Peter Diamond, Dale Mortensen, and Christopher Pissarides were awarded the Nobel Prize in 2010, is search theory, a large body of work modeling how people find and accept job offers. Search theory argues that supply and demand do not fully determine market wages. Instead, supply and demand for labor set bounds on wages. A host of factors determine where wages fall within those bounds: bargaining power, labor market institutions (including the strength of unions), and social conventions. So, search theory suggests that even explanations that make technology and globalization dominant must acknowledge that the rules matter.[28]

The third reason is that technology and globalization don't simply happen randomly, falling out of the sky like manna from heaven. Technology and globalization themselves are also shaped by the rules. Let's look at each in turn.

Technology and skills

Many economists argue that technological changes, such as the use of computers in the workplace, have shifted employers' demand for workers with different levels of technological skills, thereby driving a wedge between the wages of those at the lower end of the U.S. income scale and those at the upper end and contributing to the rise of inequality.[29] Though a popular idea, the argument that technology and skills can explain current patterns of inequality is becoming more difficult to justify.

There were early signs of problems with the technology explanation even as the theory became popular. The difference in wages paid to high- and low-skill workers expanded most rapidly during the 1980s and remained relatively stable and large in the 1990s and 2000s, the era when information and computing technology really took off.[30] The technology argument also can't predict movements in the race and gender wage gaps.[31] Nor can the rising incomes of those in the top 1 percent be explained as a matter of technology; these are driven by CEOs and finance, and would be unlikely to be affected by any skill gaps.[32]

More recent research has shown that the skills gap argument, however true it may have been in the past, has now lost much validity. The higher education premium has stalled; it has not increased over the past 10 years.[33] Highly skilled workers are taking over less-skilled occupations and face weakening career trajectories. Productivity growth remains historically slow, indicating that a massive wave of technology isn't disrupting normal business practices in much of the economy. There are also powerful arguments that a weak labor market can in some cases even deter technological change: if wages are not rising, there is less incentive to invest in labor-saving capital and technologies.[34]

This is not to say technology has had no impact on inequality, or that it won't in the future. Technological advances can provide employers with powerful new means to monitor workers and more precisely specify work tasks and set work schedules, shifting the distribution of income within businesses.[35] Technology can contribute to top income growth by creating opportunities from blue-ocean innovation, but tech can also create opportunities for businesses to exploit network effects, endowing firms with market power, able to extract high levels of rents. Whether businesses introduce labor-complementing or labor-substituting technologies in the future will depend not just on the laws of technology, but on the rules of the economy that determine how the gains from technology are distributed. Moreover, if the government chooses to impose carbon prices, more of our scarce research talent will be directed toward saving the planet, rather than saving labor.

Globalization

In the past several decades, the scale, scope, and nature of international trade in the U.S. economy have been changing, with commensurate changes wrought on businesses and workers. But this rise of globalization has also been determined and carried out through rules—rules that we have set, and rules that we have played an important role in setting internationally, and these rules have had major consequences for how globalization has played out.

There is no doubt that this deepening of global economic linkages presents tremendous opportunity for efficiencies— obtaining things we couldn't have without trade and producing things where specialization made for economic gains—innovations, and increases in general welfare. But it is also true that globalization has had significant costs, particularly in the context of the weak labor market that the United States has been experiencing. Daron Acemoglu and co-authors found that trade competition from China alone displaced a conservatively estimated 2.4 million U.S. jobs between 1999 and 2011.[36] David Autor and co-authors similarly found that Chinese import penetration of the U.S. market explained 25 percent of lost manufacturing jobs in the 1990s and 2000s, with those jobs being lost much faster than they were replaced. This had significant consequences for wage losses, extended spells of unemployment, and greater strains on public budgets for unemployment and disability insurance, early retirement, and health care costs.[37] Other researchers found that the labor share of income fell farthest in U.S. industries most exposed to import competition.[38]

Note that even in the best of circumstances, the economic argument that suggested the freeing of trade would lead to enhanced general welfare also said that, in the absence of active government policies, it would also lead to greater inequality within the U.S., as unskilled wages fell as a result of the indirect competition from the more abundant unskilled labor abroad.[39] In effect, American unskilled workers would be forced to compete with unskilled workers from emerging markets and developing countries across a range of goods and services, and this would drive down wages.[40] Even though the United States is relatively abundant in high-skill workers compared to many trading part-ner countries, more than 62 percent of the U.S. labor force still has less than a college degree, meaning we might expect trade to make a majority of Americans worse off.[41] Standard theory at best argued that the gainers could compensate the losers, but it never said that they would. While other countries recognized the risks of globalization and took offsetting actions, the United States did not.

In addition to these costs, globalization has also created opportunities for businesses to earn big rents from the restruc-turing and fragmentation of production chains across geographic regions and multiple business entities. This is also motivated by pressures from financial markets. Globalization allows firms to take advantage of differences not only in labor costs arising from wage differences, but also in costs arising from differences in regulatory standards and taxation.

This is especially important in the era of free trade agree-ments, which in reality are *managed* trade agreements. These agreements are less about trade and more about the regulatory environment corporations face investing and doing business over-seas. Providing stronger guarantees for American corporations abroad—for instance, by allowing them to sue for lost profits from government regulations using secretive international "inves-tor-state dispute settlements" rather than local democratic institu-tions—has made it even more attractive to trade internationally. One important example showing that globalization is more about rewriting the rules of the economy than about trade: trade agreements have weakened competition from generic drugs in global pharmaceutical markets drugs, which has helped drive up global pharmaceutical prices.

We see this directly with intellectual property rights, which are part of the U.S.'s system for incentivizing innovation. Poorly designed intellectual property rights regimes can not only increase monopoly power, thereby raising prices and pricing some out of the market, but can even impede innovation. The most important input in the production of research and innovation is prior and complementary knowledge.[42] Researchers and the academic community have expressed real concerns that the U.S. intellectual property regime has become unbalanced, and with trade agreements the U.S. is exporting this system to the rest of the world.

So globalization, too, is not only about an abstract and exogenous set of forces, but also about the rules we set to manage the effect of increasing global connectedness on our economic lives. And no country plays a more important role than the U.S. in setting the international rules. If we want to get the rules right on trade, we should not export parts of our economic rules that have led to rapid rises of inequality in income, wealth, and political influence at home. Most importantly for the United States, we should not expand protections that tip the balance in favor of those already winning from trade, either by creating excessively stringent intellectual property rights or by establishing a legal regime that grants investors new rights to challenge public decision-making.

ACKNOWLEDGMENTS

Rewriting the Rules had the help of a very robust team. Thank you first to Felicia Wong, President and CEO of the Roosevelt Institute, where this project was originated and supported. In addition to the Roosevelt Institute's Nell Abernathy, Adam Hersh, Susan Holmberg, and Mike Konczal, who co-authored *Rewriting the Rules*, and Eric Harris Bernstein, who served as its primary research assistant, a number of others provided important research and editorial contributions, including Andrea Flynn, Dorian Warren, and Tim Price at the Roosevelt Institute and Carola Binder at the University of California, Berkeley. The project benefited from critical strategy and media advice from Marcus Mrowka and David Palmer at the Roosevelt Institute.

Prior to the initial publication of *Rewriting the Rules*, the Roosevelt Institute solicited expert input and held a series of convenings to help shape the report. The launch event for

Rewriting the Rules, and post-launch efforts to bring the report's central message to a broader audience, have also benefited greatly from the participation, insights, and support of many experts and leaders. Thank you to the following individuals who have been a part of this process (organizations listed for affiliation purposes only): Axel Aubrun (Topos Partnership), Dean Baker (Center for Economic Policy and Research), Mark Barenberg (Columbia University School of Law), Craig Becker (AFL-CIO), Suzanne Berger (MIT), Jared Bernstein (Center on Budget and Policy Priorities), Josh Bivens (Economic Policy Institute), Kate Black (American Women), Paul Booth (AFSCME), Raphael Bostic (University of Southern California Price School), Heather Boushey (Washington Center for Equitable Growth), Beth Ann Bovino (Standard & Poor's), Julia Bowling (Brennan Center for Justice), Ellen Bravo (Family Values @ Work Consortium), David Card (University of California, Berkeley), Frank Clemente (Americans for Tax Fairness), Michael Cragg (The Brattle Group), Sheldon Danziger (Russell Sage Foundation), Mike Darner (Congressional Progressive Caucus), Hon. Bill de Blasio (Mayor, City of New York), Brad DeLong (University of California, Berkeley), David desJardins (consultant and investor), Xavier de Souza Briggs (Ford Foundation), Geert Dhondt (John Jay College of Criminal Justice), Lisa Donner (Americans for Financial Reform), Steven Fazzari (Washington University in St. Louis), Amanda Fischer (Office of Representative Maxine Waters), Sarah Fleisch Fink (National Partnership for Women and Families), Nancy Folbre (University of Massachusetts, Amherst), Rana Foroohar (*Time*), Daniel Geldon (consultant), Richard Gilbert (University of California, Berkeley), Michelle Holder (John Jay College of Criminal Justice), Olivier Giovannoni (Bard College), Stanley Greenberg (Greenberg Quinlan Rosner Research), Robert Greenstein (Center on Budget and Policy Priorities), Martin Guzman (Columbia University), Jody Heymann (University of California, Los Angeles), John Hiatt (AFL-CIO), Bart Hobijn (Federal Reserve Bank of San Francisco), Matt Hollamby (Wyss Foundation), Chye-Ching Huang (Center on Budget and Policy Priorities), Taylor Jo Isenberg (Roosevelt Institute), Arun Ivatury (SEIU), Elizabeth Jacobs (Washington Center for Equitable Growth), Seth Johnson (AFSCME), Simon Johnson (MIT Sloan School), Ianna Kachoris (MacArthur Foundation), Julie Kashen (Make It Work Campaign), Stephanie Kelton (U.S. Senate Budget Committee), Richard Kirsch (Roosevelt Institute), Steve Kreisberg (AFSCME), Anna Lefer Kuhn (Arca Foundation), Mark Levinson (SEIU), Tara Magner (MacArthur Foundation), Brad Miller (Roosevelt Institute), Larry Mishel (Economic Policy Institute), Markos Zúniga Moulitsas (DailyKos), Jessica Gordon Nembhard (John Jay College of Criminal Justice), Manuel Pastor (University of Southern California), Dan Pedrotty (AFT), Aaron Pickrell (Remington Road Group, on behalf of NYC Mayor Bill de Blasio), Kalen Pruss (Office of Martin O'Malley), Robert Reich (University of California, Berkeley), Rashad Robinson (Color of Change), Christina Romer (University of California, Berkeley), Emmanuel Saez (University of California, Berkeley), Aimee Santos-Lyons (Western States Center), Lee Saunders (AFSCME), Steve Savner (Center for Community

Change), John Schmitt (Center for Economic and Policy Research), Dan Schwerin (Office of Hillary Rodham Clinton), Adrianne Shropshire (Black Civic Engagement Fund), Zach Silk (Silk Strategic), Damon Silvers (Roosevelt Institute/AFL-CIO), Jessica Smith (AFT), Robert Solow (MIT), William Spriggs (AFL-CIO), Graham Steele (U.S. Senate Banking Committee), Lynn Stout (Cornell University Law School), Richard Trumka (AFL-CIO), Naomi Walker (AFSCME), Hon. Elizabeth Warren (U.S. Senator), Randi Weingarten (AFT), and David Woolner (Roosevelt Institute).

Special thanks to Roosevelt Institute staff, Initiative for Policy Dialogue staff, and consultants for their support and contributions: Hannah Assadi, Aman Banerji, Johanna Bonewitz, Lydia Bowers, Brenna Conway, Samantha Diaz, Renée Fidz, Joelle Gamble, Debarati Ghosh, Kathryn Greenberg, Laurie Ignacio, Jiaming Ju, Eamon Kircher-Allen, Violetta Kuzmova, Chris Linsmayer, Gabriel Matthews, Joe McManus, Camellia Phillips, Marybeth Seitz-Brown, Liz Sisson, Alan Smith, Mark Stelzner, Kevin Stump, Alexandra Tempus, Patrick Watson, and Anastasia Wilson.

Thanks, as always, to the team at W. W. Norton & Company, including Drake McFeely and Jeff Shreve, for their belief in the value of this work and their leadership in helping it reach a wider audience.

Rewriting the Rules was made possible with generous support from the Ford Foundation, the MacArthur Foundation, and Bernard L. Schwartz.

NOTES

INTRODUCTION

1. Ture, Kwame and Charles V. Hamilton. 1967. *Black Power: The Politics of Liberation in America.* New York: Vintage Books. Pogge, Thomas W. 2008. *World Poverty and Human Rights: Cosmopolitan Responsibilities and Reforms.* Cambridge: Polity.
2. John F. Kennedy Library. N.d. "JFK on the Economy and Taxes." Retrieved, May 5, 2015 (http://www.jfklibrary.org/JFK/JFK-in-History/JFK-on-the-Economy-and-Taxes.aspx).
3. Kuznets, Simon. 1955. "Economic Growth and Income Inequality." *The American Economic Review* 45(1):2-28. Some thought his observation so important that they dubbed it "Kuznets's Law." There were some theoretical reasons to expect this pattern: in early stages of development, some parts of the country were more able to take advantage of the new opportunities and pull ahead of others. Eventually the laggards catch up. Piketty, Thomas and Emmanuel Saez. 2003. "Income Inequality in the United States." *The Quarterly Journal of Economics* 68(1):1-39. Retrieved May 5, 2015 (http://eml.berkeley.edu/~saez/pikettyqje.pdf).

4. Congressional Budget Office. 2011. *Trends in the Distribution of Household Income Between 1979 and 2007.* A CBO Study, Publication No. 4043. Retrieved May 5, 2015 (http://www.cbo.gov/sites/default/files/10-25-HouseholdIncome_0.pdf).

5. Greenstone, Michael and Adam Looney. 2011. "Trends: Reduced Earnings for Men in America." *Brookings,* July 2011 Edition. Retrieved May 5, 2015 (http://www.brookings.edu/research/papers/2011/07/men-earnings-greenstone-looney).

6. Bricker, Jesse, Lisa J. Dettling, Alice Henriques, Joanne W. Hsu, Kevin B. Moore, John Sabelhaus, Jeffrey Thompson and Richard A. Windle. 2014. *Changes in U.S. Family Finances from 2010 to 2013: Evidence from the Survey of Consumer Finances.* Federal Reserve Bulletin 100(4). Retrieved May 5, 2015 (http://www.federalreserve.gov/pubs/bulletin/2014/pdf/scf14.pdf).

7. Okun, Arthur. 1975. *Equality and Efficiency: The Big Tradeoff.* Washington, DC: Brookings Institution Press.

8. The International Commission on the Measurement of Economic Performance and Social Progress pointed out that GDP did not provide a good measure of economic performance. See Stiglitz, Joseph E., Amartya Sen, and Jean-Paul Fitoussi. 2008. "Report by the Commission on the Measurement of Economic Performance and Social Progress." Presented at the plenary meeting of the Commission on the Measurement of Economic Performance and Social Progress, April 22-23, Paris, France. The IMF and other studies note, however, that even in the standard metrics of GDP growth and stability, economies with more inequality perform more poorly.

9. OECD. 2014. "Focus on Inequality and Growth." Organisation for Economic Cooperation and Development. Retrieved May 5, 2015 (http://www.oecd.org/els/soc/Focus-Inequality-and-Growth-2014.pdf).

10. *Ibid.*

11. OECD. N.d. "Income Distribution and Poverty: By Country." Organisation for Economic Cooperation and Development. Retrieved May 4, 2015 (http://stats.oecd.org/index.aspx?queryid=46189).

12. Andrews, Edmund L. 2008. "U.S. Details $800 Billion Loan Plans." *The New York Times*, November 25, 2008. Retrieved May 5, 2015 (http://www.nytimes.com/2008/11/26/business/economy/26fed. html?pagewanted=all).

13. Cynamon, Barry and Steven Fazzari. 2014. "Inequality, the Great Recession, and Slow Recovery." New York, NY: The Institute for New Economic Thinking. Retrieved May 4, 2015 (http://ineteconomics. org/sites/inet.civicactions.net/files/Cyn-Fazz%20Cons&Inequ%20 141024%20revised%20Oct.pdf). Blomquist, Daren. 2012. "2012 Foreclosure Market Outlook for CMA." Presented at the California Mortgage Association Winter Seminar, February 2, Universal City, CA. Retrieved May 4, 2015 (http://www.slideshare.net/RealtyTrac/2012-foreclosure-market-outlook-for-cma). Federal Reserve of St. Louis. "Real Median Household Income in the United States." FRED Economic Data. Retrieved May 4, 2015 (http://research.stlouisfed.org/fred2/series/MEHOINUSA672N).

14. Stiglitz, Joseph. 2015. "New Theoretical Perspectives on the Distribution of Income and Wealth among Individuals: Part I. The Wealth Residual." *NBER Working Paper No. 21189* (http://www.nber.org/papers/w21189).

15. Jiang, Yang, Mercedes Ekono, and Curtis Skinner. 2015. "Basic Facts About Low-Income Children: Children Under 18 Years, 2013." New York, NY: National Center for Children in Poverty. Retrieved May 5, 2015 (http://www.nccp.org/publications/pdf/text_1100.pdf).

16. Galbraith, John Kenneth. 1952. *American Capitalism: The Concept of Countervailing Power*. Boston, MA: Houghton Mifflin. The first financial crisis after 1929 was the S & L crisis of 1989, the result of the deregulation of the 1980s.

17. Sherman, Matthew. 2009. "A Short History of Financial Deregulation in the United States." Washington, DC: Center for Economic and Policy Research. Retrieved May 5, 2015 (http://www.cepr.net/documents/publications/dereg-timeline-2009-07.pdf). Some aspects of deregulation, such as in airlines, actually began a little earlier. Air-

line deregulation did not bring about the kind of competitive market for which the deregulators had hoped, and therefore discredited the theory of contestability underlying deregulation, but the really adverse effects of deregulation began with the deregulation of the financial system.

18. Berger, Suzanne. 2014. "How Finance Gutted Manufacturing." *The Boston Review*, April 1, 2014. Retrieved May 4, 2015 (http://bostonreview .net/forum/suzanne-berger-how-finance-gutted-manufacturing).

THE CURRENT RULES

1. Bureau of Economic Analysis. 2015. *National Income and Product Accounts Table 1.1.6.* Washington, DC: U.S. Department of Commerce. Retrieved May 5, 2015 (https://www.bea.gov/national/xls/ gdplev.xls).

2. Bureau of Labor Statistics. 2015. *Labor Force Statistics from the Current Population Survey.* Washington, DC: U.S. Department of Labor. Retrieved May 8, 2015 (http://data.bls.gov/timeseries/ LNS11300000).

3. Bureau of Economic Analysis. 2015. *Monthly Personal Income, DPI, PCE and Personal Saving: Levels and Percent Changes.* Washington, DC: U.S. Department of Commerce. Retrieved May 8, 2015 (http:// www.bea.gov/newsreleases/national/pi/2015/pdf/pi0315_hist.pdf).

4. Board of Governors of the Federal Reserve System. 2014. "Financial Accounts of the United States: Flow of Funds, Balance Sheets, and Integrated Macroeconomic Accounts." Washington, DC: U.S. Federal Reserve. Retrieved May 8, 2015 (http://www.federalreserve.gov/ releases/z1/Current/z1.pdf).

5. *Ibid.*

6. Bowles, Samuel and Herbert Gintis. 2007. "Power." UMass Amherst Economics Department Working Paper Series, Paper 37. Amherst, MA: UMass Amherst Economics Department. Retrieved May 8, 2015 (http://tuvalu.santafe.edu/~bowles/PowerWP.pdf).

7. Posner, Richard A. 1979. "The Chicago School of Antitrust Analysis." *University of Pennsylvania Law Review* 127(4):925-948. Stiglitz, Joseph E. 2001. "Information and the Change in the Paradigm in Economics." Nobel Prize Lecture. Retrieved April 15, 2015 (http://www.nobelprize.org/nobel_prizes/economic-sciences/laureates/2001/stiglitz-lecture.pdf).

8. Yergin, Daniel and Joseph Stanislaw. 2002. *The Commanding Heights: The Battle for the World Economy*. Glencoe, IL: Free Press.

9. Boldrin, Michele and David K. Levine. 2013. "The Case Against Patents." *Journal of Economic Perspectives* 27(1):3-22.

10. Moser, Petra. 2012. "Patents and Innovation: Evidence from Economic History." *Stanford Law and Economics Olin Working Paper No 437*. Retrieved May 8, 2015 (http://dx.doi.org/10.2139/ssrn.2180847).

11. Stiglitz, Joseph E. 2014. "Intellectual Property Rights, the Pool of Knowledge, and Innovation." NBER Working Paper No. 20014. The National Bureau of Economic Research. Retrieved May 4, 2015 (http://nber.org/papers/w20014).

12. *Ibid.*

13. Stiglitz, Joseph E. 2008. *The Three Trillion Dollar War*. New York: W. W. Norton. SIGAR's Office of Special Projects. 2015. "Department of Defense Spending on Afghanistan Reconstruction: Contracts Comprised $21 Billion of $66 Billion in Total Appropriations, 2002—May 2014." Washington, DC: Office of the Special Inspector General for Afghanistan Reconstruction. Retrieved May 8, 2015 (https://www.sigar.mil/pdf/special%20projects/SIGAR-15-40-SP.pdf).

14. Oliver, Thomas R., Philip R. Lee, and Helene L. Lipton. 2004. "A Political History of Medicare and Prescription Drug Coverage." *The Milbank Quarterly* 82(2):283-354. Retrieved May 8, 2015 (http://www.ncbi.nlm.nih.gov/pmc/articles/PMC2690175/). Hayford, Tamara. 2011. "Spending Patterns for Prescription Drugs Under Medicare Part D." Washington, DC: U.S. Congressional Budget Office.

15. Shapiro, Carl and Hal Varian. 1999. *Information Rules: A Strate-*

gic Guide to the Network Economy. Boston, MA: Harvard Business School Press. Cabral, Luis M.B., David J. Salant, Glenn A. Woroch. 1999. "Monopoly pricing with network externalities." *International Journal of Industrial Organization* 17(2):199-214.

16. Kroll, Luisa and Kerry A. Dolan. 2015. "The World's Billionaires." New York, NY: *Forbes Magazine.* Retrieved May 8, 2015 (http://www.forbes.com/billionaires/).

17. Stiglitz, Joseph E. 2013. *The Price of Inequality: How Today's Divided Society Endangers Our Future.* New York, NY: W. W. Norton & Company, pp. 28-52.

18. *Ibid,* pp. 39-43

19. Izadi, Elahe. 2012. "Exclusive: AHIP Gave More Than $100 Million to Chamber's Efforts to Derail Health Care Reform." *National Journal,* June 13, 2012. Retrieved May 8, 2015 (http://www.nationaljournal.com/blogs/influencealley/2012/06/exclusive-ahip-gave-more-than-100-million-to-chamber-s-efforts-to-derail-health-care-reform-13).

20. Bordo, Michael, Barry Eichengreen, Daniela Klingebiel, Maria Soledad Martinez-Peria and Andrew K. Rose. 2001. "Is the Crisis Problem Growing More Severe?" *Economic Policy* 16(32):53-82. Retrieved May 9, 2015 (http://www.nber.org/papers/w8716.pdf).

21. Luttrell, David, Tyler Atkinson, and Harvey Rosenblum. 2013. "Assessing the Costs and Consequences of the 2007-09 Financial Crisis and Its Aftermath." *Dallas Fed* 8(7):1-4. Retrieved, May 8, 2015 (http://www.dallasfed.org/assets/documents/research/eclett/2013/el1307.pdf).

22. *Op. cit. Bordo, Michael, et al.*

23. Grossman, Sanford J. and Joseph E. Stiglitz. 1980. "On the Impossibility of Informationally Efficient Markets." *The American Economic Review* 70(3):393-408. Retrieved May 8, 2015 (https://www.aeaweb.org/aer/top20/70.3.393-408.pdf). Stiglitz, Joseph E. and Bruce Greenwald. 2003. *Towards a New Paradigm in Monetary Economics.* Cambridge, UK: Cambridge University Press. Rosenblum, Harvey. 2011. "Choosing the

Road to Prosperity: Why We Must End Too Big to Fail—Now." Federal Reserve Bank of Dallas Annual Report. Retrieved May 3, 2015 (http://www.dallasfed.org/assets/documents/fed/annual/2011/ar11.pdf).

24. Johnson, Simon and James Kwak. 2011. *13 Bankers: The Wall Street Takeover and the Next Financial Meltdown*. New York, NY: Vintage.

25. *Ibid.*

26. Authors' calculations of FRED Economic Data: Federal Reserve Bank of St. Louis. 2014. "Value Added by Private Industries: Finance, Insurance, Real Estate, Rental, and Leasing: Finance and Insurance as a Percentage of GDP." St. Louis, MO: Federal Reserve Bank of St. Louis. Retrieved May 8, 2015 (https://research.stlouisfed.org/fred2/series/VAPGDPFI).

27. Philippon, Thomas and Ariell Reshef. 2009. "Wages and Human Capital in the U.S. Financial Industry: 1909–2006." *The Quarterly Journal of Economics* 127(4):1551-1609. Retrieved May 8, 2015 (http://qje.oxfordjournals.org/content/127/4/1551).

28. Bakija, Jon, Adam Cole, and Bradley T. Heim. 2012. "Jobs and Income Growth of Top Earners and the Causes of Changing Income Inequality: Evidence from U.S. Tax Return Data." Williams College and U.S. Department of the Treasury Office of Tax Analysis. Retrieved May 4, 2015 (http://web.williams.edu/Economics/wp/BakijaColeHeimJobsIncomeGrowthTopEarners.pdf).

29. *Ibid.* Bivens, Josh and Lawrence Mishel. 2013. "The Pay of Corporate Executives and Financial Professionals as Evidence of Rents in Top 1 Percent Incomes." *Journal of Economic Perspectives* 27(3):57-78.

30. *Op. cit. Philippon, Thomas, "Wages and Human Capital . . ."*

31. *Ibid.*

32. Demyanyk, Yuliya. 2006. "Time for Predatory Lending Laws." *The Regional Economist* October 2006:10-11. Retrieved May 9, 2015. (https://www.stlouisfed.org/~/media/Files/PDFs/publications/pub_assets/pdf/re/2006/d/income-inequality.pdf).

33. Lusardi, Annamaria. 2008. "Financial Literacy: An Essential Tool for Informed Consumer Choice?" Dartmouth College, Har-

vard Business School, and National Bureau of Economic Research. Retrieved May 8, 2015 (http://www.dartmouth.edu/~alusardi/ Papers/Lusardi_Informed_Consumer.pdf).

34. Grind, Kirsten. 2012. "What Libor Means for You." *The Wall Street Journal Weekend Investor.* August 3, 2012. Retrieved May 8, 2015 (http://www.wsj.com/articles/SB100008723963904435455045775 65120728037852).

35. Bray, Chad, Jenny Anderson and Ben Protess. 2014. "Big Banks Are Fined $4.25 Billion in Inquiry into Currency-Rigging." *The New York Times DealBook.* November 12, 2014. Retrieved May 8, 2015 (http:// dealbook.nytimes.com/2014/11/12/british-and-u-s-regulators-fine-big-banks-3-16-billion-in-foreign-exchange-scandal/).

36. Greenwood, Robin and David Scharfstein. 2013. "The Growth of Finance." *Journal of Economic Perspectives* 27(2):3-28. Retrieved May 8, 2015 (http://www.people.hbs.edu/dscharfstein/growth_of_ modern_finance.pdf).

37. Fama, Eugene F. and Kenneth R. French. 2010. "Luck versus Skill in the Cross-Section of Mutual Fund Returns." *The Journal of Finance* 65(5):1915-1947.

    35 percent figure: *"Thus, asset management explain 2.2 percentage points of the 6.1 percentage point increase in finance output as a share of GDP, or 36% of the growth in the ratio of financial sector output to GDP."*

38. Gorton, Gary and Andrew Metrick. 2010. "Regulating the Shadow Banking System." Washington, DC: Brookings Institution. Retrieved May 4, 2015 (http://www.brookings.edu/~/media/projects/bpea/fall-2010/2010b_bpea_gorton.pdf). Diamond, Douglas W. and Philip H. Dybvig. 1983. "Bank Runs, Deposit Insurance, and Liquidity." *The Journal of Political Economy* 91(3):401-419.

39. Levitin, Adam J. and Tara Twomey. 2011. "Mortgage Servicing." *Yale Journal on Regulation* 28(1). Retrieved May 8, 2015 (http://papers. ssrn.com/sol3/papers.cfm?abstract_id=1324023).

40. Philippon, Thomas. 2014. "Has the U.S. Finance Industry Become Less Efficient? On the Theory and Measurement of Finan-

cial Intermediation." Cambridge, MA: National Bureau of Economic Research. Retrieved May 5, 2015 (http://pages.stern.nyu.edu/~tphilipp/papers/Finance_Efficiency.pdf).

41. Cecchetti, Stephen G. and Enisse Kharroubi. 2012. "Reassessing the impact of finance on growth." BIS Working Paper No. 381. Retrieved May 8, 2015 (http://www.bis.org/publ/work381.pdf). Cecchetti, Stephen G. and Enisse Kharroubi. 2015. "Why does financial sector growth crowd out real economic growth?" BIS Working Paper No. 490. Retrieved May 8, 2015 (http://http://www.bis.org/publ/work490.pdf).

42. *Ibid.*

43. Konczal, Mike and Marcus Stanley. 2013. "An Unfinished Mission: Making Wall Street Work for Us." New York, NY: The Roosevelt Institute. Retrieved May 8, 2015 (http://rooseveltinstitute.org/sites/all/files/Unfinished_Mission_2013.pdf)

44. *Op. cit. Cecchetti, Stephen G. and Enisse Kharroubi, "Why does financial sector growth . . ."*

45. Stout, Lynn. 2012. *The Shareholder Value Myth: How Putting Shareholders First Harms Investors, Corporations, and the Public.* San Francisco, CA: Berrett-Koehler Publishers.

46. Sullivan, E. Thomas. 1988. "The Antitrust Division as a Regulatory Agency: An Enforcement Policy in Transition." Pp. 106-141 in *Public Policy toward Corporate Takeovers*, edited by Murray L. Weidenbaum and Kenneth Chilton. Edison, NJ: Transaction Publishers.

47. Holstrom, Bengt and Steven N. Kaplan. 2001. "Corporate Governance and Merger Activity in the United States: Making Sense of the 1980s and 1990s." *Journal of Economic Perspectives* 15(2):121-144.

48. Holstrom, Bengt and Steve N. Kaplan. 2003. "The State of U.S. Corporate Governance: What's Right and What's Wrong?" University of Chicago Booth School of Business and the National Bureau of Economic Research. Retrieved May 8, 2015 (http://www.chicagobooth.edu/assests/stigler/185.pdf).

49. *Op. cit. Bakija, Jon, Adam Cole, and Bradley T. Heim.*

50. Lazonick, William. 2014. "Taking Stock: Why Executive Pay Results in an Unstable and Inequitable Economy." New York, NY: The Roosevelt Institute. Retrieved May 8, 2015 (http://rooseveltinstitute.org/sites/all/files/Lazonick_Executive_Pay_White_Paper_Roosevelt_Institute.pdf).

51. Davis, Alyssa and Lawrence Mishel. 2014. "CEO Pay Continues to Rise as Typical Workers Are Paid Less." Washington, DC: Economic Policy Institute. Retrieved May 8, 2015 (http://www.epi.org/publication/ceo-pay-continues-to-rise/).

52. Holmberg, Susan and Michael Umbrecht. 2014. "Understanding the CEO Pay Debate: A Primer on America's Ongoing C-Suite Conversation." New York, NY: The Roosevelt Institute. Retrieved May 8, 2015 (http://rooseveltinstitute.org/sites/all/files/Susan_Holmberg_Michael_Umbrecht_Understanding_the_CEO_Pay_Debate_Web.pdf).

53. Almeida, Heitor, Vyacheslav Fos and Mathias Kronlund. 2014. "The Real Effects of Share Repurchases." University of Illinois at Urbana-Champaign. Retrieved May 8, 2015 (http://papers.ssrn.com/sol3/papers.cfm?abstract_id=2276156).

54. *Ibid.* Lazonick, William. 2014. "Profits Without Prosperity." Boston, MA: Harvard Business Review. Retrieved May 8, 2015 (https://hbr.org/2014/09/profits-without-prosperity).

55. Bertrand, Marianne and Sendhil Mullainathan. 2001. "Are CEO's Rewarded for Luck? The One's Without Principles Are." *The Quarterly Journal of Economics* August 2001: 901-932. Retrieved May 9, 2015 (http://web.stanford.edu/group/scspi/_media/pdf/Reference%20Media/Bertrand%20and%20Mullainathan_2001_Elites.pdf).

56. Frydman, Carola and Raven E. Saks. 2010. "Executive Compensation: A New View from a Long-Term Perspective, 1936–2005." *The Review of Financial Studies* 23(5):2099-2138.

57. DellaVigna, Stefano and Joshua M. Pollet. 2007. "Demographics and Industry Returns." *American Economic Review*, 97(5): 1667-1702 Retreived May 9, 2015 (http://eml.berkeley.edu/~sdellavi/wp/demogr07-08-23AER.pdf).

58. Asker, John, Joan Farre-Mensa and Alexander Ljungqvist. 2015. "Corporate Investment and Stock Market Listing: A Puzzle?" *Review of Financial Studies* 28(2):342-390.

59. Mason, J. W. 2015. "Disgorge the Cash: The Disconnect Between Corporate Borrowing and Investment." New York, NY: The Roosevelt Institute. Retrieved May 8, 2015 (http://rooseveltinstitute. org/sites/all/files/Mason_Disgorge_the_Cash.pdf).

   This change also has serious consequences for monetary policy, as it means that aggregate investment might have less responsiveness to changes in debt financing; see Mason 2015 "Disgorge the Cash" (http://rooseveltinstitute.org/sites/all/files/Mason_Disgorge_the_ Cash.pdf).

60. Stein, Kara M. 2015. *Toward Healthy Companies and a Stronger Economy: Remarks to the U.S. Treasury Department's Corporate Women in Finance Symposium.* U.S. Securities and Exchange Commission. Retrieved May 8, 2015 (http://www.sec.gov/news/speech/stein-toward-healthy-companies.html).

61. *Op. cit. Mason, J. W. (Authors' analysis of Federal Reserve Flow of Funds Database.)*

   For further detail see Mason 2015 "Disgorge the Cash" (http:// rooseveltinstitute.org/sites/all/files/Mason_Disgorge_the_Cash .pdf).

62. Business Insider. 2015. "BlackRock CEO Larry Fink tells the world's biggest business leaders to stop worrying about short-term results." *Business Insider,* April 14, 2015. Retrieved May 8, 2015 (http://www.businessinsider.com/larry-fink-letter-to-ceos-2015-4#ixzz3ZbDKE4oi).

63. Internal Revenue Service. 2010. *Individual Income Tax Rates and Shares, 2010.* (IRS Statistics of Income Bulletin, Winter 2013) U.S. Department of the Treasury. Retrieved May 9, 2015 (http://www.irs. gov/pub/irs-soi/13inwinbulratesshare.pdf); Internal Revenue Service. *Statistics of Income Individual Income Tax Rates and Shares.* Table 6. U.S. Department of the Treasury. Retrieved May 9, 2015 (http://

www.irs.gov/uac/SOI-Tax-Stats-Individual-Income-Tax-Rates-and-Tax-Shares#_tables).

64. Congressional Budget Office. 2011. *Trends in the Distribution of Household Income Between 1979 and 2007.* Congressional Budget Office. Retrieved May 8, 2015 (https://www.cbo.gov/sites/default/files/10-25-HouseholdIncome_0.pdf).

65. Piketty, Thomas, Emmanuel Saez, and Stefanie Stantcheva. 2014. "Optimal Taxation of Top Labor Incomes: A Tale of Three Elasticities." *American Economic Journal: Economic Policy 2014* 6(1):230–271.

66. Tax Policy Center. 2015. "U.S. Individual Income Tax: Personal Exemptions and Lowest and Highest Tax Bracket Tax Rates and Tax Base for Regular Tax, Tax Years 1913-2015." Urban Institute Tax Policy Center. Retrieved May 8, 2015 (http://www.taxpolicycenter.org/taxfacts/Content/PDF/historical_parameters.pdf).

67. Congressional Budget Office. 2013. *The Distribution of Major Tax Expenditures in the Individual Income Tax System.* Washington, DC: Congressional Budget Office. Retrieved May 8, 2015 (https://www.cbo.gov/sites/default/files/43768_DistributionTaxExpenditures.pdf).

68. *Ibid. Op cit. IRS "Individual Income Tax Rates . . . Table 6."*
    Already the second largest tax expenditure in 2011, mortgage interest deductibility—73 and 15 percent of which goes to the top quintile and top 1 percent, respectively—is expected to continue growing steeply over the next several years.

69. *Op. cit. Congressional Budget Office. "The Distribution of Major Tax Expenditures . . ."*

70. *Ibid.*

71. Transfer payments include includes cash payments from Social Security, unemployment insurance, Supplemental Security Income, Aid to Families with Dependent Children, Temporary Assistance for Needy Families, veterans' benefits, workers' compensation, and state and local government assistance programs, as well as the value of in-kind benefits, including food stamps, school lunches and break-

fasts, housing assistance, energy assistance, Medicare, Medicaid, and the Children's Health Insurance Program.

72. *Op. cit. Congressional Budget Office. "Trends in the Distribution of Household Income . . ."*

73. *Ibid.*

74. *Op. cit. Congressional Budget Office. "The Distribution of Major Tax Expenditures . . ."*

75. Toder, Eric. 2008. "Who Pays Capital Gains Tax?" The Urban Institute Tax Policy Center. Retrieved May 8, 2015 (http://www.taxpolicycenter.org/UploadedPDF/1001201_Capital_gains_tax.pdf).

76. Hungerford, Thomas L. 2011. *Changes in the Distribution of Income Among Tax Filers Between 1996 and 2006: The Role of Labor Income, Capital Income, and Tax Policy.* Congressional Research Service. Retrieved May 8, 2015 (http://taxprof.typepad.com/files/crs-1.pdf).

77. *Op. cit. Congressional Budget Office. "The Distribution of Major Tax Expenditures . . ."*

78. Internal Revenue Service. 2012. *The 400 Individual Income Tax Returns Reporting the Largest Adjusted Gross Incomes Each Year, 1992–2012.* Table 1. U.S. Department of the Treasury. Retrieved May 8, 2015 (http://www.irs.gov/pub/irs-soi/12intop400.pdf).

79. Piketty, Thomas, Emmanuel Saez, and Stefanie Stantcheva. 2014. "Optimal Taxation of Top Labor Incomes: A Tale of Three Elasticities." *American Economic Journal: Economic Policy* 6(1):230-71.

80. *Ibid.*

81. Gornick, Janet C. and Branko Milanovic. 2015. "Income Inequality in the United States in Cross-National Perspective: Redistribution Revisited." LIS Center Research Brief. Retrieved May 8, 2015 (http://www.gc.cuny.edu/CUNY_GC/media/CUNY-Graduate-Center/PDF/Centers/LIS/LIS-Center-Research-Brief-1-2015.pdf?ext=.pdf).

82. Hungerford, Thomas L. 2015. *Taxes and the Economy: An Economic Analysis of the Top Tax Rates Since 1945* (Updated). Congressional Research

Service. Retrieved May 8, 2015 (https://fas.org/sgp/crs/misc/R42729 .pdf).

83. Rothschild, Casey and Florian Scheuer. 2011. "Optimal Taxation with Rent-Seeking." NBER Working Paper No. 17035. Retrieved May 8, 2015 (http://www.nber.org/papers/w17035.pdf). Lockwood, Benjamin B. and Charles G. Nathanson. Pending. "Taxation and the Allocation of Talent" Under revision at the request of the *Journal of Political Economy* as of June 2014.

84. Ostry, Jonathan D., Andrew Berg, and Charalambos G. Tsangarides. 2014. "Redistribution, Inequality, and Growth." International Monetary Fund. Retrieved May 8, 2015 (https://www.imf.org/external/pubs/ft/sdn/2014/sdn1402.pdf).

85. Korinek, Anton and Joseph E. Stiglitz. 2008. "Dividend Taxation and Intertemporal Tax Arbitrage." NBER Working Paper No. 13858. Retrieved May 8, 2015 (http://www.nber.org/papers/w13858.pdf).

86. Yagan, Danny. 2015. "Capital Reform and the Real Economy: The Effects of the 2003 Dividend Tax Cut." NBER Working Paper No. 21003. Retrieved May 6, 2015 (http://www.nber.org/papers/w21003).

87. Conesa, Juan Carlos, Sagiri Kitao, and Dirk Krueger. 2008. "Taxing Capital? Not a Bad Idea After All!" University of Pennsylvania. Retrieved May 8, 2015 (http://economics.sas.upenn.edu/~dkrueger/research/RevisionIII.pdf).

88. Reis, Catarina. 2011. "Entrepreneurial Labor and Capital Taxation." *Macroeconomic Dynamics* 15(3):326-335. Retrieved April 8, 2015 (https://ideas.repec.org/a/cup/macdyn/v15y2011i03p326-335_00 .html). Christiansen, Vidar and Matti Tuomala. 2008. "On taxing capital income with income shifting." *International Tax and Public Finance* 15(4):527-545. Retrieved May 8, 2015 (http://eml.berkeley. edu/~saez/course/christiansen-tuomalaITAX08capitalincomeshift ing.pdf).

89. Diamond, Peter, and Emmanuel Saez. 2011. "The Case for a Progressive Tax: From Basic Research to Policy Recommendations."

Journal of Economic Perspectives 25(4): 165-90. Retrieved April 1, 2015 (http://economics.mit.edu/files/6820).

90. Full Employment and Balanced Growth Act of 1978. Public Law 95-523. 92 Stat. 1887.

The Federal Reserve's statutory objectives for monetary policy, as listed in the Federal Reserve Act of 1913, are maximum employment, stable prices, and moderate long-term interest rates, but the statute is commonly referred to as the "dual mandate."

91. Federal Reserve Bank of St. Louis. FRED Economic Data. "Interest rates, Discount Rate for United States." Retrieved May 5, 2015 (http://research.stlouisfed.org/fred2/series/INTDSRUSM193N).

92. Orszag, Peter. 2001. "How the Bush Tax Cut Compares in Size to the Reagan Tax Cuts." Center on Budget and Policy Priorities. Retrieved May 8, 2015 (http://www.cbpp.org/archives/2-6-01tax2.htm).

93. Bernanke, Ben S. and Frederic S. Mishkin. 1997. "Inflation Targeting: A New Framework for Monetary Policy?" *American Economic Association* 11(2):97-116. Retrieved April 10, 2015 (http://web.uconn.edu/ahking/BernankeMishkin97.pdf). Batini, Nicoletta, Kenneth Kuttner, and Douglas Laxton. 2005. "Does Inflation Targeting Work in Emerging Markets?" International Monetary Fund. Retrieved May 5, 2015 (http://www.imf.org/external/pubs/ft/weo/2005/02/pdf/chapter4.pdf).

94. Bernanke, Ben S. 2003. "A Perspective on Inflation Targeting." Public Address at the Annual Washington Policy Conference of the National Association of Business Economists, Washington, DC. Retrieved May 1, 2015 (http://www.federalreserve.gov/BoardDocs/speeches/2003/20030325/default.htm).

"The Federal Reserve, though rejecting the inflation-targeting label, has greatly increased its credibility for maintaining low and stable inflation, has become more proactive in heading off inflationary pressures, and has worked hard to improve the transparency of its policymaking process—all hallmarks of the inflation-targeting approach."

95. Friedman, Milton. 1976. "Inflation and Unemployment." Nobel

Memorial Lecture, The University of Chicago. Retrieved May 8, 2015 (http://socjologia.amu.edu.pl/isoc/userfiles/40/friedman-lecture.pdf). Ball, Laurence and N. Gregory Mankiw. 2002. "The NAIRU in Theory and Practice." *Journal of Economic Perspectives* 16(4):115-136. Retrieved May 8, 2015 (http://www.scholar.harvard.edu/files/mankiw/files/jep.ballmankiw.pdf).

96. Storm, Servass and C. W. M. Naastepad. 2013. "How Milton Friedman's NAIRU Has Increased Inequality, Damaging Innovation and Growth." Institute for New Economic Thinking. Retrieved May 1, 2015 (http://ineteconomics.org/blog/institute/how-milton-friedman-s-nairu-has-increased-inequality-damaging-innovation-and-growth). Krueger, Alan B., Judd Cramer, and David Cho. 2014. "Are the Long-Term Unemployed on the Margins of the Labor Market?" Brookings Papers on Economic Activity. The Brookings Institute. Retrieved May 1, 2015 (http://www.brookings.edu/~/media/Projects/BPEA/Spring%20 2014/2014a_Krueger.pdf).

97. Fisher, Irving. 1933. *The Debt-Deflation Theory of Great Depressions.* Federal Reserve Bank of St. Louis. Retrieved April 1, 2015 (https://fraser.stlouisfed.org/docs/meltzer/fisdeb33.pdf).

98. Baker, Dean and Jared Bernstein. 2013. "Getting Back to Full Employment: A Better Bargain for Working People." Washington, DC: Center for Economic and Policy Research. Retrieved May 4, 2015 (http://www.cepr.net/documents/Getting-Back-to-Full-Employment_20131118.pdf).

99. *Ibid.*

100. Carpenter, Seth B. and William M. Rodgers III. 2004. "The Disparate Labor Market Impacts of Monetary Policy." *Journal of Policy Analysis and Management* 23(4):813-830.

101. Furman, Jason and Joseph E. Stiglitz. 1998. "Economic Consequences of Income Inequality." Presented at the Income Inequality Issues and Policy Options Symposium, August 27-29, Jackson Hole, WY. Retrieved May 4, 2015 (http://www.kc.frb.org/publicat/sympos/1998/S98stiglitz.pdf).

102. Blinder, Alan. 2014. "Petrified Paychecks." *Washington Monthly.* Retrieved March 30, 2015 (http://www.washingtonmonthly.com/magazine/novemberdecember_2014/features/petrified_paychecks 052713.php?page=all).

103. Oreopoulous, Philip, Till von Wachter and Andrew Heisz. 2006. "The Short- and Long-Term Career Effects of Graduating in a Recession: Hysteresis and Heterogeneity in the Market for College Graduates." National Bureau of Economic Research Working Paper No. 12159. Retrieved May 4, 2015 (http://www.nber.org/papers/w12159).

104. Federal Reserve Bank of St. Louis. 2015. "Employment Level— Part-Time for Economic Reasons, All Industries." FRED Economic Database. Retrieved May 8, 2015 (http://research.stlouisfed.org/fred2/series/LNS12032194).

105. Markham, Jerry W. 2002. *A Financial History of the United States: From Christopher Columbus to the Robber Barons (1492-1900).* Armonk, NY: M.E. Sharpe.

106. Kirsch, Richard. 2015. "The Future of Work in America: Policies to Empower American Workers and Secure Prosperity for All." The Roosevelt Institute. Retrieved May 4, 2015 (http://rooseveltinstitute. org/policy-and-ideas/big-ideas/report-future-work-america-policies-empower-american-workers-and-secure-p).

107. Greenhouse, Steven. 2013 "VW and Its Workers Explore a Union at a Tennessee Plant." *The New York Times.* Retrieved May 1, 2015. (http://www.nytimes.com/2013/09/07/business/vw-and-auto-workers-explore-union-at-tennessee-plant.html?_r=0).

108. Bureau of Labor Statistics. 2015. *Union Members—2014. Union Membership Annual News Release.* Retrieved May 4, 2015 (http://www.bls.gov/news.release/union2.htm).

109. The State of Working America. 2012. "Cumulative change in total economy productivity and real hourly compensation of production/nonsupervisory workers, 1948-2013." Economic Policy Institute. Retrieved May 5, 2015 (http://www.stateofworkingamerica.org/chart/swa-wages-figure-4u-change-total-economy/).

Authors' analysis: Data are for production and non-supervisory workers, accounting for roughly 80 percent of all employees in the U.S.

110. Godard, John. 2003. "Do Labor Laws Matter? The Density Decline and Convergence Thesis Revisited." *Industrial Relations*, 42:458-492. Retrieved May 4, 2015 (http://papers.ssrn.com/sol3/papers.cfm?abstract_id=416152). Labour Program, Government of Canada. 2014. "Union Coverage in Canada, 2013." Retrieved May 4, 2015 (http://www.labour.gc.ca/eng/resources/info/publications/union_coverage/union_coverage.shtml).

111. OECD. 2014. "Economic Policy Reforms 2014: Going for Growth Interim Report." Organisation for Economic Co-operation and Development. Retrieved May 4, 2015. (http://www.keepeek.com/Digital-Asset-Management/oecd/economics/economic-policy-reforms-2014_growth-2014-en#page1).

112. *Op. cit. Kirsch, Richard.*

113. Hacker, Jacob S. and Paul Pierson. 2011. *Winner-Take-All Politics*. New York, NY: Simon & Schuster. Retrieved April 3, 2015 (http://polisci2.ucsd.edu/ps126aa/documents/HackerPierson2010.pdf).

114. Bernhardt, Annette, Ruth Milkman, Nik Theodore, Douglas Heckathorn, Mirabai Auer, James DeFilippis, Ana Luz Gonzalez, Victor Narro, Jason Perelshteyn, Diana Polson, and Michael Spiller. 2009. "Broken Laws, Unprotected Workers: Violations of Employment and Labor Laws in America's Cities." New York, NY: National Employment Law Project. Retrieved May 5, 2015 (http://nelp.org/content/uploads/2015/03/BrokenLawsReport2009.pdf).

115. Barenberg, Mark. 2015. "Widening the Scope of Worker Organizing: Legal Reforms to Facilitate Multi-Employer Organizing, Bargaining, and Striking." New York, NY: Roosevelt Institute, forthcoming.

116. *Harris et al. v. Quinn, Governor of Illinois, et al.* No. 11-681.

117. Card, David, Thomas Lemieux, and W. Craig Riddell. 2003. "Unions and the Wage Inequality: A Comparative Study of the U.S.,

the U.K., and Canada." The National Bureau of Economic Research Working Paper No. 9473. Retrieved May 8, 2015 (http://www.nber. org/papers/w9473).

118. Western, Bruce and Jake Rosenfeld. 2011. "Unions, Norms, and the Rise in U.S. Wage Inequality." *American Sociological Review*, 76(4):513-537.

119. Gittleman, Maury and Brooks Pierce. 2007. "New Estimates of Union Wage Effects in the US." *Economics Letters* 95(2):198-202. Retrieved May 5, 2015 (http://econpapers.repec.org/article/eeeecolet/ v_3a95_3ay_3a2007_3ai_3a2_3ap_3a198-202.htm).Buchmueller, Thomas C, John DiNardo and Robert G. Valletta. 2002. "Union Effects on Health Insurance Provision and Coverage in the United States." *Industrial and Labor Relations Review* 55(4):610-627. Retrieved May 5, 2015 (http://www-personal.umich.edu/~jdinardo/Pubs/bdv2002.pdf).

120. Schmitt, John, Margy Waller, Shawn Fremstad and Ben Zipperer. 2007. "Unions and Upward Mobility for Low-Wage Workers." Washington, DC: Center for Economic and Policy Research. Retrieved May 8, 2015 (http://www.cepr.net/documents/publications/unions-low-wage-2007-08.pdf).

121. The State of Working America. 2012. "Share of workers with paid leave, by wage group, 2011." Economic Policy Institute. Retrieved May 5, 2015 (http://www.stateofworkingamerica.org/chart/swa-wages-table-4-12-share-workers-paid/). Bureau of Labor Statistics. 2010. "Table 32. Defined Benefit Plans: Summer of Plan Provisions, Private Industry Workers, National Compensation Survey, 2010." Washington, DC: U.S. Department of Labor. Retrieved May 5, 2015 (http://www.bls.gov/ncs/ebs/detailedprovisions/2010/ownership/ private/table32a.pdf).

122. OECD. 2014. "Coverage for Health Care." *Society at a Glance 2014: OECD Social Indicators*, pp. 130-131. Retrieved May 5, 2015 (http:// www.oecd-ilibrary.org/docserver/download/8113171ec026.pdf?expi res=1430514022&id=id&accname=guest&checksum=AD91A71BD 436CABD82EC75D6F53EB84A).

123. Duke, Brendan V. 2014. "America's Incredible Shrinking Overtime Rights Need an Update." Washington, DC: Center for American Progress. Retrieved May 5, 2015 (https://cdn.americanprogress.org/wp-content/uploads/2014/06/OvertimeRights-REVISEDFINAL2.pdf).

124. Cooper, David. 2015. "Given the Economy's Growth, the Federal Minimum Wage Could Be Significantly Higher." Washington, DC: Economic Policy Institute. Retrieved May 9, 2015 (http://www.epi.org/publication/given-the-economys-growth-the-federal-minimum-wage-could-be-significantly-higher/).

125. Cooper, David, Lawrence Mishel, and John Schmitt. 2015. "We Can Afford a $12.00 Federal Minimum Wage in 2020." Economic Policy Institute Briefing Paper #398. Retrieved May 9, 2015 (http://www.epi.org/publication/we-can-afford-a-12-00-federal-minimum-wage-in-2020/).

126. Weil, David. 2014. *The Fissured Workplace.* Cambridge, MA: Harvard University Press.

127. *Op. cit. Bernhardt, Annette, et al.*

128. Meixell, Brady and Ross Eisenbrey. 2014. "An Epidemic of Wage Theft is Costing Workers Hundreds of Millions of Dollars a Year." Washington, DC: Economic Policy Institute. Retrieved May 9, 2015 (http://www.epi.org/publication/epidemic-wage-theft-costing-workers-hundreds/).

129. Passel, Jeffrey S. and D'Vera Cohn. 2015. "Share of Unauthorized Immigrant Workers in Production, Construction Jobs Falls Since 2007." Washington, DC: Pew Research Center. Retrieved May 9, 2015 (http://www.pewhispanic.org/2015/03/26/share-of-unauthorized-immigrant-workers-in-production-construction-jobs-falls-since-2007/). Pastor, Manuel, Justin Scoggins, Vanessa Carter, and Jared Sanchez. 2014. "Citizenship Matters: How Children of Immigrants Will Sway the Future of Politics." Washington, DC: Center for American Progress. Retrieved May 8, 2015 (https://cdn.americanprogress.org/wp-content/uploads/2014/07/CitizenshipMatters-report.pdf).

130. United States Census Bureau. N.d. *Historical Poverty Tables—People* Table 2. U.S. Department of Commerce. Retrieved May 9, 2015 (http://www.census.gov/hhes/www/poverty/data/historical/people.html).

131. DiNardo, John, Nicole M. Fortin, and Thomas Lemieux. 1996. "Labor Market Institutions and the Distribution of Wages, 1973-1992: A Semiparametric Approach." *Econometrica* 64(5):1001-1044. Manning, Alan (2003). *Monopsony in Motion: Imperfect Competition in Labor Markets*. Princeton, NJ: Princeton University Press.

132. Dube, Arindrajit. 2013. "Minimum Wages and the Distribution of Family Incomes." Working Paper. Retrieved May 9, 2015 (https://dl.dropboxusercontent.com/u/15038936/Dube_MinimumWagesFamilyIncomes.pdf).

133. Autor, David, Alan Manning and Christopher L. Smith. 2015. "The Contribution of the Minimum Wage to U.S. Wage Inequality Over Three Decades: A Reassessment." National Bureau of Economic Research Working Paper No. 16533. Retrieved May 9, 2015 (http://www.nber.org/papers/w16533). Dutta-Gupta, Indivar. 2014. "Improving Wages, Improving Lives: Why Raising the Minimum Wage Is a Civil and Human Rights Issue." Washington, DC: Center on Poverty and Inequality, Georgetown Law School. Retrieved May 9, 2015 (http://civilrightsdocs.info/pdf/reports/Minimum-Wage-Report-FOR-WEB.pdf). *Op. cit. Autor, David, Alan Manning, and Christopher L. Smith.*

134. Jacobs, Ken, Ian Perry and Jenifer MacGillvary. 2015. "The High Public Cost of Low Wages." UC Berkeley Labor Center. Retrieved May 5, 2015 (http://laborcenter.berkeley.edu/the-high-public-cost-of-low-wages/).

135. Allegretto, Sylvia, Marc Doussard, Dave Graham-Squire, Ken Jacobs, Dan Thompson, and Jeremy Thompson. 2013. "Fast Food, Poverty Wages: The Public Cost of Low-Wage Jobs in the Fast-Food Industry." University of California, Berkeley, Center for Labor Research and Education and the University of Illinois at

Urbana-Champaign Department of Urban & Regional Planning. Retrieved May 5, 2015 (laborcenter.berkeley.edu/pdf/2013/fast_food_poverty_wages.pdf).

136. Henly, Julia R. and Susan J. Lambert. 2014. "Unpredictable Work Timing in Retail Jobs: Implications for Employee Work-Life Conflict." *Industrial & Labor Relations Review* 67(3):986-1016. Retrieved May 5, 2015 (http://ssascholars.uchicago.edu/work-scheduling-study/files/industrial__labor_relations_review-2014-henly-986-1016.pdf). Woolf, Steven H. and Paula Braveman. 2011. "Where Health Disparities Begin: The Role of Social and Economic Determinants—And Why Current Policies May Make Matters Worse." *Health Affairs* 30(10):1852-1859. Retrieved May 5, 2015 (http://content.healthaffairs.org/content/30/10/1852.short).

137. Kalleberg, Arne L., Barbara Reskin, and Ken Hudson. 2000. "Bad Jobs in America: Standard and Nonstandard Employment Relations and Job Quality in the United States." *American Sociological Review* 65(2):256-278. Retrieved May 9, 2015 (http://www.uark.edu/ua/yangw/CaliforniaLaborData/Research/kalleberg2000.pdf).

138. Lynch, Robert and Patrick Oakford. 2013. "The Economic Effects of Granting Legal Status and Citizenship to Undocumented Immigrants." Washington, DC: Center for American Progress. Retrieved May 5, 2015 (https://cdn.americanprogress.org/wp-content/uploads/2013/03/EconomicEffectsCitizenship-1.pdf).

139. Taylor, Paul and D'Vera Cohn. 2012. "A Milestone En Route to a Major Minority Nation." Washington, DC: Pew Research Center. Retrieved May 9, 2015 (http://www.pewsocialtrends.org/2012/11/07/a-milestone-en-route-to-a-majority-minority-nation/).

140. Katznelson, Ira. 2006. *When Affirmative Action Was White.* New York: W. W. Norton & Company.

141. Woolner, David. N.d. "African Americans and the New Deal: A Look Back in History." New York, NY: The Roosevelt Institute. Retrieved May 5, 2015 (http://www.rooseveltinstitute.org/new-roosevelt/african-americans-and-new-deal-look-back-history).

142. DeWitt, Larry. 2010. "The Decision to Exclude Agricultural and Domestic Workers from the 1935 Social Security Act." *Social Security Bulletin* 70(4). U.S. Social Security Administration Office of Retirement and Disability Policy. Retrieved May 5, 2015 (http://www.ssa. gov/policy/docs/ssb/v70n4/v70n4p49.html).

143. Logan, John R. 2011. "Separate and Unequal: The Neighborhood Gap for Blacks, Hispanics and Asians in Metropolitan America." US2010 Project. Retrieved May 5, 2015 (http://www.s4.brown.edu/ us2010/Data/Report/report0727.pdf).

144. Alexander, Michelle. 2011. "The New Jim Crow." *Ohio State Journal of Criminal Law* 9(1):7-26. Retrieved May 8, 2015 (http://moritzlaw. osu.edu/osjcl/Articles/Volume9_1/Alexander.pdf).

145. U.S. Department of Education Office for Civil Rights. March 2014. *Data Snapshot: School Discipline* (Issue Brief No. 1). Washington, DC: U.S. Department of Education. Retrieved May 5, 2015 (https:// www2.ed.gov/about/offices/list/ocr/docs/crdc-discipline-snapshot. pdf).The Sentencing Project. N.d. "Fact Sheet: Trends in U.S. Corrections." Retrieved May 9, 2015 (http://sentencingproject.org/doc/ publications/inc_Trends_in_Corrections_Fact_sheet.pdf).

146. Passel, Jeffrey S. and D'Vera Cohn. 2014. "Unauthorized Immigrant Totals Rise in 7 States, Fall in 14: Decline in Those From Mexico Fuels Most State Decreases." Washington, DC: Pew Research Center's Hispanic Trends Project. Retrieved May 5, 2015 (http://www. pewhispanic.org/2014/11/18/unauthorized-immigrant-totals-rise-in-7-states-fall-in-14/). *Op. cit. Pastor, Manuel, Justin Scoggins, Vanessa Carter, and Jared Sanchez.*

147. Passel, Jeffrey S. and D'Vera Cohn. 2011. "Unauthorized Immigrant Population: National and State Trends, 2010." Washington, DC: Pew Research Center. Retrieved May 9, 2015 (http://www.pewhispanic. org/files/reports/133.pdf).

148. *Op. Cit. Lynch, Robert and Patrick Oakford.*

149. Authors' analysis: Bureau of Labor Statistics. 2015. *Labor Force Statistics from the Current Population Survey.* U.S. Department of Labor.

Retrieved April 29, 2015 (http://www.bls.gov/webapps/legacy/cpsatab2.htm).

150. Hellerstein, Judith K. and David Neumark. 2008. "Workplace Segregation in the United States: Race, Ethnicity, and Skill." *The Review of Economics and Statistics* 90(3):459-477. Retrieved May 5, 2015 (http://www.socsci.uci.edu/~dneumark/H&NRESTAT.pdf).

151. Bronfenbrenner, Kate and Dorian T. Warren. 2007. "Race, Gender, and the Rebirth of Trade Unionism." Retrieved May 9, 2015 (http://digitalcommons.ilr.cornell.edu/cgi/viewcontent.cgi?article=1839&context=articles).

152. Ture, Kwame and Charles V. Hamilton. 1967. *Black Power: The Politics of Liberation in America.* New York: Vintage Books. Pogge, Thomas W. 2008. *World Poverty and Human Rights: Cosmopolitan Responsibilities and Reforms.* Cambridge, MA: Polity.

153. Pager, Devah, Bruce Western and Bart Bonikowski. 2009. "Discrimination in a Low-Wage Labor Market: A Field Experiment." *American Sociological Review* 74(5):777-799.

154. The Annie E. Casey Foundation. 2014. "Kids Count: Data Book State Trends in Child Well-Being." Retrieved May 5, 2015 (http://www.aecf.org/m/resourcedoc/aecf-2014kidscountdatabook-2014.pdf).

155. Data First. "What Is the Poverty Level of Our School(s)?" Center for Public Education. Retrieved May 5, 2015 (http://www.data-first.org/data/what-is-the-poverty-level-of-our-schools/).

156. *Op. cit. United States Census Bureau Historical Poverty Tables—People.* Macartney, Suzanne, Alemayehu Bishaw, and Kayla Fontenothttp. *2013 Poverty Rates for Selected Detailed Race and Hispanic Groups by State and Place: 2007-2011.* American Community Survey Briefs. Washington, DC: United States Department of Commerce. Retrieved May 9, 2015 (http://www.census.gov/prod/2013pubs/acsbr11-17.pdf). CLASP. 2013. "Child Poverty in the U.S." CLASP, Washington, DC. Retrieved May 9, 2015 (http://www.clasp.org/resources-and-publications/publication-1/9.18.13-CensusPovertyData_FactSheet.pdf).

157. Kochhar, Rakesh and Richard Fry. 2014. "Wealth Inequality Has

Widened Along Racial, Ethnic Lines Since End of Great Recession." Washington, DC: Pew Research Center. Retrieved May 5, 2015 (http://www.pewresearch.org/fact-tank/2014/12/12/racial-wealth-gaps-great-recession/).

158. Shapiro, Thomas M. and Melvin L. Oliver. 2006. *Black Wealth/White Wealth* (2nd ed.). New York, NY: Taylor & Francis.

159. *Op. cit. Kochhar, Rakesh and Richard Fry.*

160. Shapiro, Thomas, Tatjana Meschede, and Sam Osoro. 2013. "The Roots of the Widening Racial Wealth Gap: Explaining the Black-White Economic Divide." Waltham, MA: Institute on Assets & Social Policy, Brandeis University. Retrieved May 5, 2015 (http://iasp.brandeis.edu/pdfs/Author/shapiro-thomas-m/racialwealthgapbrief.pdf).

161. *Op. cit. Shapiro, Thomas and Melvin Oliver.*

162. *Op. cit. Kochhar, Rakesh and Richard Fry.*

163. Mauer, Marc and Ryan S. King. 2007. "Uneven Justice: State Rates of Incarceration By Race and Ethnicity." Washington, DC: The Sentencing Project. Retrieved May 5, 2015 (http://www.sentencingproject.org/doc/publications/rd_stateratesofincbyraceandethnicity.pdf).

164. The Pew Charitable Trusts. 2010. "Collateral Costs: Incarceration's Effect on Economic Mobility." Washington, DC: The Pew Charitable Trusts. Retrieved May 4, 2015 (http://www.pewtrusts.org/~/media/legacy/uploadedfiles/pcs_assets/2010/CollateralCosts1pdf.pdf).

165. *Op. cit. Alexander, Michelle.*

166. *Op. cit. DeWitt.*

167. *Op. cit. The Pew Charitable Trusts.*

168. Neal, Derek and Armin Rick. 2013. "The Prison Boom & the Lack of Black Progress after Smith & Welch." Chicago, IL: University of Chicago Becker Friedman Institute. Retrieved May 5, 2015 (https://econresearch.uchicago.edu/sites/econresearch.uchicago.edu/files/Prison%20Boom.pdf).

169. Benner, Chris and Manuel Pastor. 2014. "Brother, Can You Spare Some Time? Sustaining Prosperity and Social Inclusion in America's Metropolitan Regions." *Urban Studies* September 5, 2014 Edition.

Retrieved May 10, 2015 (http://usj.sagepub.com/content/early/2014/09/03/0042098014549127.abstract).

170. Council of Economic Advisors. 2014. *Nine Facts About American Families and Work.* Washington, DC: Executive Office of the President. Retrieved May 10, 2015 (https://www.whitehouse.gov/sites/default/files/docs/nine_facts_about_family_and_work_real_final.pdf).

171. Federal Reserve Bank of St. Louis. 2015. "Civilian Labor Force Participation Rate—Women." FRED Economic Database. Retrieved May 8, 2015 (http://research.stlouisfed.org/fred2/series/LNS11300002). OECD. 2013. "Female Participation Rate in OECD Regions." Organization for Economic Cooperation and Development. Retrieved May 1, 2015 (http://rag.oecd.org/media/rag/stories/data/Gender.pdf)

172. Glynn, Sarah Jane. 2012. "Fact Sheet: Paid Family and Medical Leave: Updated Labor Standards Could Help U.S. Workers Make Ends Meet." Washington, DC: Center for American Progress. Retrieved April 2, 2015 (http://www.americanprogress.org/issues/labor/news/2012/08/16/11980/fact-sheet-paid-family-and-medical-leave).

173. U.S. Department of Labor. 2010. "Women in the Labor Force in 2010." Retrieved May 9, 2015 (http://www.dol.gov/wb/factsheets/Qf-laborforce-10.htm). Washington, DC: National Women's Law Center. 2014. "Underpaid & Overloaded: Women in Low-Wage Jobs." Retrieved May 9, 2015 (http://www.nwlc.org/sites/default/files/pdfs/final_nwlc_lowwagereport2014.pdf).

174. Warren, Dorian T. 2015. "Putting Families First: Good Jobs for All." Center for Community Change. Retrieved, April 30, 2014 (http://www.goodjobsforall.org/wp-content/uploads/2015/05/PFA-GJFA-Launch-Report.pdf). Hegewisch, Ariane and Heidi Hartmann. 2014. "Occupational Segregation and the Gender Wage Gap: A Job Half Done." Washington, DC: Institute for Women's Policy Research. Retrieved May 8, 2014 (http://www.iwpr.org/publications/pubs/occupational-segregation-andthe-gender-wage-gap-a-job-half-done/at_download/file).

175. *Ibid.*

176. National Partnership for Women & Families. 2011. "Everyone Gets Sick. Not Everyone Has Time to Get Better: A Briefing Book on Establishing a Paid Sick Days Standard." Washington DC: National Partnership for Women & Families. Retrieved May 5, 2015 (http://go.nationalpartnership.org/site/DocServer/PSD_Briefing_Book.pdf?docID=9121).

177. Ben-Ishai, Liz. 2015. "The Serious Consequences of Lack of Paid Leave." Washington, DC: CLASP. Retrieved May 5, 2015 (http://www.clasp.org/resources-and-publications/publication-1/2015-02-03-FMLA-Anniversary-Brief.pdf).

178. Oxfam America and Hart Research Associates. 2013. "Hard Work, Hard Lives: Survey Exposes Harsh Realities Faced by Low-Wage Workers in the U.S." Boston, MA: Oxfam America. Retrieved May 5, 2015 (http://www.oxfamamerica.org/static/media/files/low-wage-worker-report-oxfam-america.pdf).

179. Raub, Amy, Tina-Marie Assi, Elise Vaughn Winfrey, Alison Earle, Gonzalo Moreno, Gabriella Kranz, Ilona Vincent, Arijit Nandi and Jody Heymann. 2014. "Labor Policies to Promote Equity: Findings from 197 Countries and Beijing Platform Signatories." Los Angeles, CA: WORLD Policy Analysis Center. Retrieved May 9, 2015 (http://worldpolicyforum.org/sites/default/files/WORLD_Policy_Brief_Labor_Policies_to_Promote_Equity_at_Work_and_at_Home_2015.pdf).

180. Frost, Jennifer J. and Laura Duberstein Lindberg. 2013. "Reasons for Using Contraception: Perspectives of US Women Seeking Care at Specialized Family Planning Clinics." *Contraception* 87(4):465-472. Retrieved May 1, 2015 (http://www.guttmacher.org/pubs/journals/j.contraception.2012.08.012.pdf).

181. National Women's Center. 2015. "Reproductive Health Is Part of the Economic Health of Women and Their Families." Washington, DC: National Women's Center. Retrieved May 5, 2015 (http://www.nwlc.org/sites/default/files/pdfs/reproductive_health_is_part_of_the_economic_health_of_women_2.18v2pdf.pdf).

182. Bailey, Martha J. 2013. "Fifty Years of Family Planning: New Evidence on the Long-Run Effects of Increasing Access to Contraception." National Bureau for Economic Research Working Paper No. 19493. Retrieved April 13, 2015 (http://www.nber.org/papers/w19493.pdf).

183. Simmons, Adelle, Katherine Warren, and Kellyann McClain. 2015. "The Affordable Care Act: Advancing the Health of Women and Children." Washington, DC: Department of Health and Human Services, Office of the Assistant Secretary for Planning and Evaluation. Retreived May 9, 2015, (http://aspe.hhs.gov/health/reports/2015/MCH/ib_mch.pdf).

184. National Women's Law Center. 2015. "Closing the Wage Gap is Crucial for Women of Color and Their Families." NWLC Fact Sheet. Retrieved May 9, 2015 (http://www.nwlc.org/resource/closing-wage-gap-crucial-women-color-and-their-families). National Women's Law Center. 2013. "50 Years & Counting: The Unfinished Business of Achieving Fair Pay." Retrieved, May 9, 2015 (http://www.nwlc.org/resource/50-years-counting-unfinished-business-achieving-fair-pay).

185. Hartmann, Heidi, Jeff Hayes, and Jennifer Clark. 2014. "How Equal Pay for Working Women Would Reduce Poverty and Grow the American Economy." Institute for Women's Policy Research Briefing Paper #C411. Retrieved May 5, 2015 (http://www.iwpr.org/publications/pubs/how-equal-pay-for-working-women-would-reduce-poverty-and-grow-the-american-economy).

186. Elborgh-Woytek, Katrin, Monique Newiak, Kalpana Kochhar, Stefania Fabrizio, Kangni Kpodar, Philippe Wingender, Benedict Clements, and Gerd Schwartz. 2013. "Women, Work, and the Economy: Macroeconomic Gains from Gender Equity." IMF Staff Discussion Note, September 2013. Retrieved May 9, 2015.

187. Aguirre, DeAnne, Leila Hoteit, Christine Rupp, and Karim Sabbagh. 2012. "Empowering the Third Billion. Women and the World of Work in 2012." Booz and Company. *Op. cit. Hartmann, Heidi, Jeff Hayes, and Jennifer Clarke.*The White House Council on Women and Girls. 2012. "Keeping America's Women Moving Forward." Washington, DC:

Executive Office of the President. Retreieved May 9, 2015 (https://www.whitehouse.gov/sites/default/files/email-files/womens_report_final_for_print.pdf).

REWRITING THE RULES

1. U.S. Government Accountability Office. 2012. "Research on Savings from Generic Drug Use." GAO-12-371R. Retrieved May 5, 2015 (http://www.gao.gov/products/GAO-12-371R).
2. Human Rights Watch. 2015. "Work Faster or Get Out: Labor Rights Abuses in Cambodia's Garment Industry." Retrieved May 8, 2015 (http://features.hrw.org/features/HRW_2015_reports/Cambodia_Garment_Workers/index.html). Platzer, Michaela D. 2014. *U.S. Textile Manufacturing and the Trans-Pacific Partnership Negotiations.* Congressional Research Service, Report No. R42772. Retrieved May 8, 2015 (https://www.fas.org/sgp/crs/row/R42772.pdf).
3. Goldman, Dana P. and Elizabeth A. McGlynn. 2005. "U.S. Health Care: Facts About Cost, Access, and Quality." Santa Monica, CA: RAND Corporation. Retrieved May 8, 2015 (https://www.rand.org/content/dam/rand/pubs/corporate_pubs/2005/RAND_CP484.1.pdf).
4. Congressional Budget Office. 2007. *Prescription Drug Pricing in the Private Sector.* CBO Paper Pub. No. 2703. Washington, DC: The Congress of the United States. Retrieved May 8, 2015 (https://www.dol.gov/ebsa/pdf/CBO010711.pdf).
5. Oliver, Thomas R., Philip R. Lee and Helene L. Lipton. 2004. "A Political History of Medicare and Prescription Drug Coverage. *The Milbank Quarterly* 82(2):283-354. Retrieved May 8, 2015 (http://www.ncbi.nlm.nih.gov/pmc/articles/PMC2690175/).
6. Himmelstein, David U., Deborah Thorne, Elizabeth Warren, and Steffie Woolhandler. 2009. "Medical Bankruptcy in the United States, 2007: Results of a National Study." *The American Journal of Medicine* 20(10):1-6. Retrieved May 8, 2015 (http://www.pnhp.org/new_bankruptcy_study/Bankruptcy-2009.pdf).

7. Financial Stability Board. 2014. "Global Shadow Banking Monitoring Report 2014." Basel, CH: Financial Stability Board. Retrieved May 5, 2015 (http://www.financialstabilityboard.org/wp-content/uploads/r_141030.pdf?page_moved=1).

8. Systemic Risk Council. 2014. "Statement by Sheila Bair on SEC's Money Fund Rules." Statement to the SEC meeting on July 23, 2014. Retrieved May 5, 2015 (http://www.systemicriskcouncil.org/2014/07/statement-by-sheila-bair-on-secs-money-fund-rules/).

9. Americans for Financial Reform. 2014. "RE: Docket No. R-1476; RIN 7100-AE08; Extensions of Credit by Federal Reserve Banks." Letter to the Board of Governors of the Federal Reserve System. Retrieved May 5, 2015 (http://ourfinancialsecurity.org/blogs/wp-content/ourfinancialsecurity.org/uploads/2014/03/AFR-Comment-On-Federal-Reserve-Emergency-Lending-Proposal.pdf).

10. Barth, Mark H. and Marco Blanco. 2003. "US Regulatory and Tax Considerations for Offshore Funds." *The Capital Guide to Hedge Funds* 118-160. Retrieved May 8, 2015 (http://www.curtis.com/siteFiles/Publications/D2CA07A14CA94DFC1DAAD5293970E197.pdf).

11. Greenwood, Robin and David Scharfstein. 2013. "The Growth of Finance." *Journal of Economic Perspectives* 27(2):3-28. Retrieved May 8, 2015 (http://www.people.hbs.edu/dscharfstein/growth_of_modern_finance.pdf).

12. Bowden, Andrew J. 2014. "Spreading Sunshine in Private Equity." Speech to the Private Equity International Private Fund Compliance Forum, May 6, 2014, New York, NY. Retrieved May 5, 2015 (http://www.sec.gov/News/Speech/Detail/Speech/1370541735361).

13. Garrett, Brandon L. 2014. *Too Big to Jail.* Cambridge, MA: Belknap Press. Rakoff, Jed S. 2014. "The Financial Crisis: Why Have No High Level Executives Been Prosecuted?" *The New York Review of Books.* Retrieved May 9, 2015 (http://www.nybooks.com/articles/archives/2014/jan/09/financial-crisis-why-no-executive-prosecutions/).

14. United States Government Accountability Office. 2011. "401(K) Plans: Improved Regulation Could Better Protect Participants from

Conflicts of Interest." Washington, DC: United States Government Accountability Office. Retrieved May 5, 2015 (http://www.gao.gov/assets/320/315363.pdf).

15. There's evidence that CEOs use buybacks when they'd otherwise miss earnings per share targets, an unproductive economic activity that directly benefits the CEO and should not be encouraged. The SEC should reexamine its rule providing "safe harbor" for buyback against charges of stock-price manipulation. Almeida, Heitor, Vyacheslav Fos, and Mathias Kronlund. 2013. "The Real Effects of Share Repurchases." Retrieved May 9, 2015 (https://www.business.illinois.edu/halmeida/repo.pdf).

16. Stiglitz, Joseph E. 1989. "Using Tax Policy to Curb Speculative Short-Term Trading." *Journal of Financial Services Research* 3(2/3):101–115. Retrieved May 5, 2015 (http://academiccommons.columbia.edu/item/ac:159631).

17. Stout, Lynn A. 1995. "Are Stock Markets Costly Casinos? Disagreement, Market Failure, and Securities Regulation." *Cornell Law Faculty Publications* Paper 751. Retrieved, April 4, 2015, (http://scholarship.law.cornell.edu/cgi/viewcontent.cgi?article=2319&context=facpub).

18. Matheson, Thornton. 2011. "Taxing Financial Transactions: Issues and Evidence." International Monetary Fund Working Paper No. 11/54. Washington: International Monetary Fund. Retrieved May 5, 2015 (https://www.imf.org/external/pubs/cat/longres.aspx?sk=24702.0).

19. Persaud, Avinash. 2012. "The Economic Consequences of the EU Proposal for a Financial Transaction Tax." *Intelligence Capital*. Retrieved May 8, 2015 (http://www.stampoutpoverty.org/wp-content/uploads/2012/10/The-Economic-Consequences-of-the-EU-Proposal-for-a-Financial-Transaction-Tax-3.pdf).

20. Bolton, Patrick and Frédéric Samama. 2012. "L-Shares: Rewarding Long-Term Investors." ECGI—Finance Working Paper No. 342/2013. Retrieved May 8, 2015 (http://papers.ssrn.com/sol3/papers.cfm?abstract_id=2188661).

21. Organisation for Economic Co-Operation and Development.

2008. "Growing Unequal?: Income Distribution and Poverty in OECD Countries." Retrieved May 8, 2015 (http://www.oecd.org/unitedstates/41528678.pdf).

22. Piketty, Thomas, Emmanuel Saez, Stefanie Stantcheva. 2011. "Optimal Taxation of Top Labor Incomes: A Tale of Three Elasticities." NBER Working Paper No. 17616. Cambridge, MA: National Bureau of Economic Research. Retrieved May 5, 2015 (http://www.nber.org/papers/w17616.pdf).

23. Stiglitz, Joseph E. 2014. "Reforming Taxation to Promote Growth and Equity." New York, NY: Roosevelt Institute. Retrieved May 8, 2015 (http://www.rooseveltinstitute.org/reforming-taxation-promote-growth-and-equity).

24. This analysis is based on the authors' calculation of projected universal pre-K costs and 2012 public postsecondary spending and tuition data from: Ginder, Scott A. and Janice E. Kelly-Reid. 2013. "Enrollment in Postsecondary Institutions, Fall 2012; Financial Statistics, Fiscal Year 2012; Graduation Rates, Selected Cohorts, 2004-09; and Employees in Postsecondary Institutions, Fall 2012." Institute of Education Sciences National Center for Education Statistics. Retrieved, April 15, 2015 (http://nces.ed.gov/pubs2013/2013183.pdf). Holt, Alex. 2008. "Doing the Math: The Cost of Publicly Funded 'Universal' Pre-K." New America Foundation. Retrieved May 5, 2015 (http://earlyed.newamerica.net/blogposts/2013/doing_the_math_the_cost_of_publicly_funded_universal_pre_k-80821).

25. Internal Revenue Service. 2010. *Individual Income Tax Rates and Shares, 2010.* IRS Statistics of Income Bulletin. Washington, DC: Internal Revenue Service. Monaghan, Angela. 2014. "US Wealth inequality—top 0.1% worth as much as the bottom 90%." New York, NY: *The Guardian.* Retrieved May 5, 2015 (http://www.theguardian.com/business/2014/nov/13/us-wealth-inequality-top-01-worth-as-much-as-the-bottom-90).

26. Marr, Chuck and Chye-Ching Huang. 2015. "President's Capital Gains Tax Proposals Would Make Tax Code More Efficient and Fair."

Washington, DC: Center on Budget and Policy Priorities. Retrieved May 9, 2015 (http://www.cbpp.org/cms/index.cfm?fa=view&id=5260).

27. Congressional Budget Office. 2013. "The Distribution of Major Tax Expenditures in the Individual Income Tax System." Washington, DC: Congress of the United States, Congressional Budget Office. Retrieved May 4, 2015 (https://www.cbo.gov/sites/default/files/43768_DistributionTaxExpenditures.pdf). Congressional Budget Office. 2011. "Trends in the Distribution of Household Income Between 1979 and 2007." A CBO Study, Publication No. 4043. Retrieved May 5, 2015 (http://www.cbo.gov/sites/default/files/10-25-HouseholdIncome_0.pdf).

28. Stiglitz, Joseph E. 2014. "Reforming Taxation to Promote Growth and Equity." New York, NY: Roosevelt Institute. Retrieved May 8, 2015 (http://www.rooseveltinstitute.org/reforming-taxation-promote-growth-and-equity).

29. George, Henry. 1935. *Progress and Poverty*. New York: Robert Schalkenbach Foundation. Retrieved May 8, 2015 (https://mises.org/sites/default/files/Progress%20and%20Poverty_3.pdf).

30. FRED Economic Data. 2015. "Civilian Labor Force Participation Rate." St. Louis, MO: Federal Reserve Bank of St. Louis. Retrieved May 8, 2015 (http://research.stlouisfed.org/fred2/series/CIVPART).

31. Carpenter, Seth B. and William M. Rodgers III. 2004. "The Disparate Labor Market Impacts of Monetary Policy." *Journal of Policy Analysis and Management* 23(4):813-830.

32. Ball, Laurence. 2014. "The Case for a Long-Run Inflation Target of Four Percent." IMF Working Paper 14/92. Washington, DC: International Monetary Fund. Retrieved May 5, 2015 (https://www.imf.org/external/pubs/ft/wp/2014/wp1492.pdf).

33. Yellen, Janet L. 2013. "A Painfully Slow Recovery for America's Workers: Causes, Implications, and the Federal Reserve's Response." Public Address. Retrieved, May 1, 2015 (http://www.federalreserve.gov/newsevents/speech/yellen20130211a.htm).

34. Schwab, Klaus and Xavier Sala-i-Martin. 2014. "The Global Competi-

tiveness Report 2014–2015: Full Data Edition." New York, NY: World Economic Forum USA. Retrieved May 5, 2015 (http://www3.weforum. org/docs/WEF_GlobalCompetitivenessReport_2014-15.pdf).

35. National Economic Council and the President's Council of Economic Advisors. 2014. "An Economic Analysis of Transportation Infrastructure Investment." Washington, DC: The White House. Retrieved May 5, 2015 (https://www.whitehouse.gov/sites/default/ files/docs/economic_analysis_of_transportation_investments.pdf).

36. Silvers, Damon. Forthcoming infrastructure report. New York: Roosevelt Institute.

37. American Society of Civil Engineers. 2013. "Transit: 2013 Report Card for America's Infrastructure." Retrieved May 8, 2015 (http:// www.infrastructurereportcard.org/a/#p/transit/overview).

38. Federal Highway Administration. 2014. *2013 Status of the Nation's Highways, Bridges, and Transit: Conditions & Performance.* U.S. Department of Transportation, Federal Highway Administration. Retrieved May 9, 2015 (http://www.fhwa.dot.gov/policy/2013cpr/ lb_es.htm).

39. Kirsch, Richard. 2015. "The Future of Work in America: Policies to Empower American Workers and Secure Prosperity for All." The Roosevelt Institute. Retrieved May 4, 2015 (http://rooseveltinstitute. org/policy-and-ideas/big-ideas/report-future-work-america-policies-empower-american-workers-and-secure-p).

40. Hartman, Mitchell. 2014. "Labor Wins Two Rulings, Walmart Vows to Fight Back." *Marketplace.* Retrieved May 9, 2015 (http://www. marketplace.org/topics/wealth-poverty/labor-wins-two-rulings-walmart-vows-fight-back).

41. Beach, Ben and Kathleen Mulligan-Hansel. 2015. "Public Goods Strategy Policy Brief." Forthcoming paper for Roosevelt Institute Future of Work Initiative. Johnson, Olatunde. 2015. "Promoting Racial and Ethnic Inclusion in Employment Through Regulatory Mandates and Incentives." Forthcoming paper for Roosevelt Institute Future of Work Initiative.

42. Bernhardt, Annette, Ruth Milkman, Nik Theodore, Douglas Heck-athorn, Mirabai Auer, James DeFilippis, Ana Luz Gonzalez, Victor Narro, Jason Perelshteyn, Diana Polson, and Michael Spiller. 2009. "Broken Laws, Unprotected Workers: Violations of Employment and Labor Laws in America's Cities." National Employment Law Project. Retrieved May 5, 2015 (http://nelp.org/content/uploads/2015/03/BrokenLawsReport2009.pdf).

43. Levin, Myron, Stuart Silverstein, and Lilly Fowler. 2014. "Pay Violations Rampant in Low-Wage Industries Despite Enforcement Efforts." Investigate West, August 27, 2014. Retrieved May 6, 2015 (http://www.invw.org/article/pay-violations-rampant-in-1468).

44. Midland, David and Keith Miller. 2013. "Raising the Minimum Wage Would Boost the Incomes of Millions of Women and Their Families." Washington, DC: Center for American Progress Action Fund. Retrieved May 6, 2015 (https://www.americanprogressaction.org/issues/labor/news/2013/12/09/80484/raising-the-minimum-wage-would-boost-the-incomes-of-millions-of-women-and-their-families/).

45. Shierholz, Heidi. 2014. "It's Time to Update Overtime Pay Rules." Washington, DC: Economic Policy Institute. Retrieved May 8, 2015 (http://www.epi.org/publication/ib381-update-overtime-pay-rules/).

46. *Ibid.*

47. Alexander, Michelle. 2011. "The New Jim Crow." *Ohio State Journal of Criminal Law* 9(1):7-26. Retrieved May 8, 2015 (http://moritzlaw.osu.edu/osjcl/Articles/Volume9_1/Alexander.pdf).

48. Henrichson, Christian and Ruth Delaney. 2012. "The Price of Prisons: What Incarceration Costs Taxpayers." New York, NY: Vera Institute of Justice, Center on Sentencing and Corrections. Retrieved May 9, 2015 (http://www.vera.org/files/price-of-prisons-maine-factsheet.pdf). Geller, Amanda, Irwin Garfinkel and Bruce Western. 2006. "The Effects of Incarceration on Employment and Wages: An Analysis of the Fragile Families Survey." Princeton, NJ: Princeton University Center for Research on Child Wellbeing. Retrieved May 9,

2015 (http://www.saferfoundation.org/files/documents/Princeton-Effect%20of%20Incarceration%20on%20Employment%20and%20Wages.pdf).

49. Schmitt, John and Kris Warner. 2010. "Ex-offenders and the Labor Market." Washington, DC: Center for Economic and Policy Research. Retrieved May 8, 2015 (http://www.cepr.net/documents/publications/ex-offenders-2010-11.pdf).

50. Saris, Patti B., William B. Carr, Jr., Ketanji B. Jackson, Ricardo H. Hinojosa, Beryl A. Howell, Dabney L. Friedrich, Jonathan J. Wroblewski, and Isaac Fulwood, Jr. 2011. "Statistical Overview of Mandatory Minimum Penalties." Pp. 119-148 in *Report to the Congress: Mandatory Minimum Penalties in the Federal Criminal Justice System*. United States Sentencing Commission. Retrieved May 6, 2015 (http://www.ussc.gov/sites/default/files/pdf/news/congressional-testimony-and-reports/mandatory-minimum-penalties/20111031-rtc-pdf/Chapter_07.pdf).

51. Giovanni, Thomas and Roopal Patel. 2013. "*Gideon* at 50: Three Reforms to Revive the Right to Counsel." New York, NY: The Brennan Center for Justice, NYU School of Law. Retrieved May 5, 2015 (http://www.brennancenter.org/sites/default/files/publications/Gideon_Report_040913.pdf).

52. Pastor, Manuel, Justin Scoggins, Vanessa Carter, and Jared Sanchez. 2014. "Citizenship Matters: How Children of Immigrants Will Sway the Future of Politics." Washington, DC: Center for American Progress. Retrieved May 8, 2015 (https://cdn.americanprogress.org/wp-content/uploads/2014/07/CitizenshipMatters-report.pdf).

53. Smith, Rebecca and Eunice Hyunhye Cho. 2013. "Workers' Rights on ICE: How Immigration Reform Can Stop Retaliation and Advance Labor Rights." New York, NY: The National Employment Law Project. Retrieved May 8, 2015 (http://www.nelp.org/content/uploads/2015/03/Workers-Rights-on-ICE-Retaliation-Report.pdf).

54. *Ibid.*

55. National Partnership for Women & Families. 2015. "The Family and

Medical Insurance Leave Act (The FAMILY Act)." Washington DC: National Partnership for Women & Families. Retrieved May 5, 2015 (http://www.nationalpartnership.org/research-library/work-family/paid-leave/family-act-fact-sheet.pdf).

56. Ray, Rebecca. 2008. "A Detailed Look at Parental Leave Policies in 21 OECD Countries." Washington, DC: Center for Economic and Policy Research. Retrieved May 5, 2015 (http://www.lisdatacenter.org/wp-content/uploads/parent-leave-details1.pdf).

57. Dagher, R. K., P. M. McGovern, and B. E. Down. 2013. "Maternity Leave Duration and Postpartum Mental and Physical Health: Implications for Leave Policies." *Journal of Health Politics, Policy and Law* 39(2):369-416. *Op. cit.* National Partnership for Women & Families. Hegewisch, Ariane and Yuko Hara. 2013. "Maternity, Paternity, and Adoption Leave in the United States." IWPR Working Paper #A143. Washington, DC: Institute for Women's Policy Research. Retrieved May 5, 2015 (http://www.iwpr.org/publications/pubs/maternity-paternity-and-adoption-leave-in-the-united-states-1).

58. Blau, Francine D. and Lawrence M. Kahn. 2013. "Female Labor Supply: Why Is the US Falling Behind?" Discussion Paper No. 7140. Bonn, DE: Institute for the Study of Labor. Retrieved May 5, 2015 (http://ftp.iza.org/dp7140.pdf). Rossin-Slater, Maya, Christopher J. Ruhm and Jane Waldfogel. 2011. "The Effects of California's Paid Family Leave Program on Mothers' Leave-Taking and Subsequent Labor Market Outcomes." NBER Working Paper No. 11715. Cambridge, MA: National Bureau of Economic Research. Retrieved May 5, 2015 (http://www.nber.org/papers/w17715.pdf).

59. Bassanini, Andrea. 2008. "The Impact of Labour Market Policies on Productivity in OECD Countries." *International Productivity Monitor* 17(2008):3-15. Retrieved May 8, 2015 (http://www.csls.ca/ipm/17/IPM-17-bassanini.pdf).

60. *Op. cit.* The National Partnership for Women & Families.

61. National Women's Law Center. 2015. "Closing the Wage Gap Is Crucial for Women of Color and Their Families." NWLC Fact Sheet.

Retrieved May 9, 2015 (http://www.nwlc.org/resource/closing-wage-gap-crucial-women-color-and-their-families). National Women's Law Center. 2013. "50 Years & Counting: The Unfinished Business of Achieving Fair Pay." Retrieved, May 9, 2015 (http://www.nwlc.org/sites/default/files/pdfs/final_nwlc_equal_pay_report.pdf).

62. Frost, Jennifer J., Adam Sonfield, Mia R. Zolna, and Lawrence B. Finer. 2014. "Return on Investment: A Fuller Assessment of the Benefits and Cost Savings of the US Publicly Funded Family Planning Program." *The Milbank Quarterly* 92(4):667-720. Retrieved May 6, 2015 (http://www.guttmacher.org/pubs/journals/MQ-Frost_1468-0009.12080.pdf).

63. Jiang, Yang, Mercedes Ekono, and Curtis Skinner. 2015. "Basic Facts About Low-Income Children: Children Under 18 Years, 2013." New York, NY: National Center for Children in Poverty. Retrieved May 5, 2015 (http://www.nccp.org/publications/pdf/text_1100.pdf).

64. Paulsell, Diane, Sarah Avellar, Emily Sama Martin, and Patricia Del Grosso. 2010. *Home Visiting Evidence of Effectiveness Review: Executive Summary*. Office of Planning, Research and Evaluation, Administration for Children and Families, US Department of Health and human Services. Retrieved May 8, 2015 (http://homvee.acf.hhs.gov/HomVEE_Executive_Summary.pdf).

65. Olds, D. L., C. R. Henderson, Jr., R. Tatelbaum and R. Chamberlin. 1988. "Improving the Life-Course Development of Socially Disadvantaged Mothers: A Randomized Trial of Nurse Home Visitation." *American Journal of Public Health* 78(11):1436-1445. Kitzman H., D. L. Olds, C. R. Henderson, Jr., C. Hanks, R. Cole, R. Tatelbaum, K. M. McConnochie, K. Sidora, D. W. Luckey, D. Shaver, K. Engelhardt, D. James and K. Barnard. 1997. "Effect of Prenatal and Infancy Home Visitation by Nurses on Pregnancy Outcomes, Childhood Injuries, and Repeated Childbearing: A Randomized Controlled Trial." *Journal of the American Medical Association* 278(8):644-652.

66. Kirkland, Kristen and Susan Mitchell-Herzfeld. 2012. *Evaluating the Effectiveness of Home Visiting Services in Promoting Children's Adjust-*

ment to School. New York State Office of Children and Family Services, Bureau of Evaluation and Research. Retrieved May 8, 2015 (http://www.pewtrusts.org/~/media/legacy/uploadedfiles/pcs_assets/2013/SchoolReadinessexecutivesummarypdf.pdf). Borkowski, John G. and Jaelyn R. Farris. 2013. "An Early, Intensive Parenting Intervention to Prevent Child Neglect: Five Year Mother-Child Outcomes." Retrieved May 8, 2015 (http://www.pewtrusts.org/~/media/legacy/uploadedfiles/pcs_assets/2013/MyBabyandMeexecutivesummarypdf.pdf).Olds, David L., Harriet Kitzman, Carole Hanks, Robert Cole, Elizabeth Anson, Kimberly Sidora-Arcoleo, Dennis W. Luckey, Charles R. Henderson Jr., John Holmberg, Robin A. Tutt, Amanda J. Stevenson, and Jessica Bondy. 2007. "Effects of Nurse Home Visiting on Maternal and Child Functioning: Age-9 Follow-up of a Randomized Trial." *Pediatrics* 120(4) e832-e845. Retrieved May 8, 2015 (http://pediatrics.aappublications.org/content/120/4/e832.abstract?sid=a49d862c-9af24f77-b005-4bececf908c3).

67. Waldfogel, Jane. 2010. "Tackling Child Poverty & Improving Child Well-Being: Lessons From Britain." Washington, DC: First Focus. Retrieved May 5, 2015 (http://fcd-us.org/sites/default/files/First%20Focus%20-%20Tackling%20Child%20Poverty.pdf).

68. Warren, Dorian T. 2015. "Putting Families First: Good Jobs for All." Washington, DC: Center for Community Change. Retrieved May 6, 2015 (http://www.scholarsstrategynetwork.org/sites/default/files/families-first-report.pdf).

69. Federal Reserve Bank of St. Louis. 2014. "Gross Federal Debt as Percent of Gross Domestic Product." FRED Economic Data. Retrieved May 8, 2015 (https://research.stlouisfed.org/fred2/series/GFDGDPA188S).

70. Chopra, Rohit. 2013. *Student Debt Swells, Federal Loans Now Top a Trillion.* Consumer Financial Protection Bureau. Retrieved May 8, 2015 (http://www.consumerfinance.gov/newsroom/student-debt-swells-federal-loans-now-top-a-trillion/).

71. Darolia, Rajeev and Dubravka Ritter. 2015. "Do Student Loan Borrowers Opportunistically Default? Evidence from Bankruptcy

Reform." Federal Reserve Bank of Philadelphia Research Department Working Paper No. 15-17. Retrieved May 5, 2015 (https://www.philadelphiafed.org/research-and-data/publications/working-papers/2015/wp15-17.pdf).

72. United States Senate Health, Education, Labor and Pensions Committee. 2012. "For Profit Higher Education: The Failure to Safeguard the Federal Investment and Ensure Student Success." Majority Committee Staff Report and Accompanying Minority Committee Staff Views. Retrieved May 8, 2015 (http://www.help.senate.gov/imo/media/for_profit_report/PartI-PartIII-SelectedAppendixes.pdf).

73. U.S. Department of Education. 2014. *Obama Administration Takes Action to Protect Americans from Predatory, Poor-Performing Career Colleges*. Washington, DC: U.S. Department of Education. Retrieved May 8, 2015 (http://www.ed.gov/news/press-releases/obama-administration-takes-action-protect-americans-predatory-poor-performing-career-colleges).

74. Evans, Melanie. 2014. "Consolidation creating giant hospital systems." Modern Healthcare, June 21, 2014. Retrieved May 5, 2015 (http://www.modernhealthcare.com/article/20140621/MAGAZINE/306219980). Murray, Robert and Suzanne F. Delbanco. 2012. "Provider Market Power in the U.S. Health Care Industry: Assessing its Impact and Looking Ahead." Catalyst for Payment Reform. Retrieved May 8, 2105 (http://www.catalyzepaymentreform.org/images/documents/Market_Power.pdf). American Medical Association. 2008. "Competition in health insurance: A comprehensive study of U.S. Markets: 2008 update." The Division of Economic and Health Policy Research, American Medical Association.

75. Levy, Jenna. 2015. "In U.S., Uninsured Rate Dips to 11.9% in First Quarter." Gallup. Retrieved May 8, 2015 (http://www.gallup.com/poll/182348/uninsured-rate-dips-first-quarter.aspx).

76. Dafny, Leemore, Jonathan Gruber, and Christopher Ody. 2014. "More Insurers Lower Premiums: Evidence from Initial Pricing in Health Insurance Marketplaces." Evanston, IL: Kellogg School of Man-

agement, Northwestern University. Retrieved May 6, 2015 (http://www.kellogg.northwestern.edu/faculty/dafny/personal/Documents/Publications/Dafny%20Gruber%20Ody%209.26.14.pdf).

77. Leyba, Mike, Michael Young, Mike Lapham, and Steve Schnapp. 2015. "State of the Dream 2015: Underbanked and Overcharged." Boston, MA: United for a Fair Economy. Retrieved May 8, 2015 (http://faireconomy.org/sites/default/files/SOTD15.pdf).

78. Freddie Mac. 2015. "Freddie Mac Update." Retrieved May 6, 2015 (http://www.freddiemac.com/investors/pdffiles/investor-presentation.pdf).

79. Hiltonsmith, Robert. 2012. "The Retirement Savings Drain: Hidden & Excessive Costs of 401(k)s." New York, NY: Demos. Retrieved May 8, 2015 (http://www.demos.org/publication/retirement-savings-drain-hidden-excessive-costs-401ks).

80. *Op. cit. Greenwood and Scharfstein.*

81. Drutman, Lee and Ethan Phelps-Goodman. 2011. "The Political One Percent of the One Percent." Washington, DC: The Sunlight Foundation. Retrieved May 5, 2015 (http://sunlightfoundation.com/blog/2011/12/13/the-political-one-percent-of-the-one-percent/). Gilens, Martin. 2014. *Affluence and Influence: Economic Inequality and Political Power in America.* Princeton, NJ: Princeton University Press.

82. McElwee, Sean. 2014. "Why the Voting Gap Matters." New York, NY: Demos. Retrieved May 5, 2015 (http://www.demos.org/sites/default/files/publications/Voters&NonVoters.pdf).

APPENDIX

1. Author's analysis of Bureau of Labor Statistics data, Average Hourly Earnings of Production and Nonsupervisory Employees: Total Private, Consumer Price Index for All Urban Consumers; U.S. Census Bureau Historical Income Data tables F-6. The BLS earnings measure covers roughly 80 percent of U.S. workers and tracks closely

to measures of median wages. We note that average compensation has increased faster than wage earnings—this is largely due to rising costs of employer-provided health insurance. Because this means employers pay more for the same benefits, growth in employee compensation does not indicate an increase in living standards.

2. U.S. Census Bureau. *Historical Poverty Tables: Table 18. Workers as a Proportion of All Poor People: 1978 to 2006.* Retrieved May 9, 2015 (http://www.census.gov/hhes/www/poverty/data/historical/hstpov18.xls).

3. Economic Policy Institute. 2012. "Annual Hours Worked by Married Men and Women Age 25-54 with Children, by Income Group, Selected Years, 1979-2010." *The State of Working America.* Retrieved May 9, 2015 (http://www.stateofworkingamerica.org/chart/swa-income-table-2-17-annual-hours-work-married/).

4. Author's analysis of:Economic Policy Institute. 2014. "Cumulative change in Total Economy Productivity and Real Hourly Compensation of production/nonsupervisory workers, 1948-2013." *State of Working America.* Retrieved May 9, 2015 (http://www.epi.org/chart/swa2014-wages-figure-4u-cumulative-change-in-total-economy-productivity-and-real-hourly-compensation-of-productionnonsupervisory-workers-1948-2013/).

5. Bureau of Labor Statistics. 2015. *News Release: The Employment Situation—April 2015.* Bureau of Labor Statistics, U.S. Department of Labor. Retrieved May 9, 2015 (http://www.bls.gov/news.release/pdf/empsit.pdf).

6. Bureau of Labor Statistics. 2015. *Charting the Labor Market: Data from the current Population Survey (CPS).* Bureau of Labor Statistics, U.S. Department of Labor. Retrieved May 9, 2015 (http://www.bls.gov/web/empsit/cps_charts.pdf).

7. Federal Reserve Bank of St. Louis. 2015. "Employment Level—Part-Time for Economic Reasons, All Industries." FRED Economic Data. Retrieved May 9, 2015 (http://research.stlouisfed.org/fred2/series/LNS12032194).

8. Bivens, Josh and Lawrence Mishel. 2013. "The Pay of Corporate Executives and Financial Professionals as Evidence of Rents in Top

1 Percent of Incomes." *Journal of Economic Perspectives.* Volume 27 (3): pp. 57-78. Retrieved May 9, 2015 (http://pubs.aeaweb.org/doi/pdfplus/10.1257/jep.27.3.57).

9. Giovannoni, Olivier. 2014. "What Do We Know About the Labor Share and the Profit Share? Part III: Measures and Structural Factors." Levy Economics Institute Working Paper No. 805.

10. Gornick, Janet and Branko Milanovic. 2015. "Income Inequality in the United States in Cross National Perspective: Re-distribution Revisited." Luxembourg Income Study Center Research Brief. May 4, 2015. Retrieved May 9, 2015 (http://www.gc.cuny.edu/CUNY_GC/media/CUNY-Graduate-Center/PDF/Centers/LIS/LIS-Center-Research-Brief-1-2015.pdf?ext=.pdf).

11. *Ibid.*

12. Causa, Oresetta and Asa Johansson. 2010. "Intergenerational Social Mobility in OECD Countries." *OECD Journal: Economic Studies* Volume 2010. Retrieved May 9. 2015 (http://www.oecd.org/eco/growth/49849281.pdf).

13. Economic Policy Institute. 2012. "Share of Families in the Bottom and Top Income Fifths in 1994 Ending Up in Various Income Fifths in 2004." *State of Working America.* Retrieved May 9, 2015 (http://www.stateofworkingamerica.org/chart/swa-mobility-figure-3b-share-families-bottom/). Acs, Gregory and Seth Zimmerman. 2008. "U.S. Intragenerational Economic Mobility from 1984 to 2004: Trends and Implications." Philadelphia, PA: Economic Mobility Project, Pew Charitable Trusts. Retrieved May 9, 2015 (http://www.urban.org/sites/default/files/alfresco/publication-pdfs/1001226-U-S-Intragenerational-Economic-Mobility-From-to--.PDF).

14. Corak, Miles. 2013. "Income Inequality, Equality of Opportunity, and Intergenerational Mobility." *Journal of Economic Perspectives* 27(3):79-102.

15. Hilger, Nathaniel G. 2015. "The Great Escape: Intergenerational Mobility Since 1940." Working Paper. Retrieved May 9, 2015 (https://drive.google.com/file/d/0B8J_qdFYwNJ6ZHY4UTRiZldIVkk/view).

16. Chetty, Raj, Nathaniel Hendren, Patrick Kline and Emmanuel Saez.

2014. "Where Is the Land of Opportunity? The Geography of Inter-generational Mobility in the United States." National Bureau of Economic Research Working Paper No. 19843. Retrieved May 9, 2015 (http://www.nber.org/papers/w19843).

17. *Ibid.*

18. Cingano, Federico. 2014. "Trends in Income Inequality and Its Impact on Economic Growth." OECD Social, Employment and Migration Working Papers No. 163. Retrieved May 9, 2015 (http://www.oecd.org/els/soc/trends-in-income-inequality-and-its-impact-on-economic-growth-SEM-WP163.pdf).

19. Chen, Alice, Emily Oster and Heidi Williams. 2014. "Why Is Infant Mortality Higher in the US than in Europe?" National Bureau of Economic Research Working Paper No. 20525. Retrieved May 9, 2015 (http://www.nber.org/papers/w20525). McKinsey & Company. 2009. "The Economic Impact of the Achievement Gap in America's Schools." McKinsey & Company, Social Sector Office. Retrieved May 9, 2015 (http://silvergiving.org/system/files/achievement_gap_report.pdf). House, James S. and David R. Williams. 2003. "Chapter Three: Understanding and Reducing Socioeconomic and Racial/Ethnic Disparities in Health." *Health and Social Justice: Politics, Ideology, and Inequity in the Distribution of Disease,* pp. 89-131, edited by Richard Hofrichter. San Francisco: Jossey-Bass. Retrieved May 9, 2015 (http://www.isr.umich.edu/williams/All%20Publications/DRW%20pubs%202003/understanding%20and%20reducing%20SE.pdf).

20. Currie, Janet. 2011. "Inequality at Birth: Some Causes and Consequences." National Bureau of Economic Research Working Paper No. 16798. Retrieved May 9, 2015 (http://www.nber.org/papers/w16798).

21. Heckman, James and Dimitriy Masterov. 2007. "The Productivity Argument for Investing in Young Children." *Review of Agricultural Economics* 29(3):446-93.

22. Burchinal, Robert. 2000. "Relating Quality of Center-Based Child Care to Early Cognitive and Language Development Longitudinally." *Child Development* 71(2):338-57. McCartney, Kathleen, Eric

Dearing, Beck A. Taylor and Kristen L. Bub. 2007. "Quality Child Care Supports the Achievement of Low-Income Children: Direct and Indirect Pathways through Caregiving and the Home Environment." *Journal of Applied Developmental Psychology* 28(5-6):411-26.

23. Duncan, Greg J. and Richard J. Murnane, editors. 2011. *Whither Opportunity? Rising Inequality, Schools, and Children's Life Changes.* New York: Russell Sage Foundation.

24. Melchior, Maria, Jean-Francois Chastang, Bruno Falisard, Cédric Galéra, Richard E. Tremblay, Sylvana M. Coté and Michel Boivin. 2012. "Food Insecurity and Children's Mental Health: A Prospective Birth Cohort Study." *PLOS ONE* 7(12):e52615. Retrieved May 9, 2015 (http://www.ncbi.nlm.nih.gov/pmc/articles/PMC3530436/).

25. Schulman, Karen. 2000. "The High Cost of Child Care Puts Quality Care out of Reach for Many Families." Washington, DC: Children's Defense Fund.

26. Turner, Margery Austin and Karina Fortuny. 2009. "Residential Segregation and Low-Income Working Families." Washington, DC: The Urban Institute. *Low-Income Working Families* Paper 10. Retrieved May 9, 2015 (http://www.urban.org/sites/default/files/alfresco/publication-pdfs/411845-Residential-Segregation-and-Low-Income-Working-Families.PDF).

27. Frank, Robert. 2005. "Positional Externalities Cause Large and Preventable Welfare Losses." *American Economic Review* 95(2):137-41. Retrieved May 9, 2015 (https://www.aeaweb.org/assa/2005/0108_1015_0601.pdf).

28. Diamond, Peter A. 2010. "Unemployment, Vacancies, Wages." Nobel Prize Lecture, December 8, 2010. Retrieved May 9, 2015 (http://www.nobelprize.org/nobel_prizes/economic-sciences/laureates/2010/diamond-lecture.pdf). Atkinson, Anthony B. 2015. Inequality: What Can Be Done? Pp 90-93. Cambridge, MA: Harvard University Press.

29. Acemoglu, Daron and David Autor. 2010. "Skills, Tasks and Technologies: Implications for Employment and Earnings." National Bureau of Economic Research Working Paper 16082. Retrieved May

9, 2015 (http://www.nber.org/papers/w16082). Autor, David H., Lawrence F. Katz and Melissa S. Kearney. 2007. "Trends in U.S. Wage Inequality: Revising the Revisionists." *The Review of Economics and Statistics* 90(2):300-323. Retrieved May 9, 2015 (http://economics.mit.edu/files/580). Autor, David H., Lawrence F. Katz and Alan B. Krueger. 1998. "Computing Inequality: Have Computers Changed the Labor Market?" *The Quarterly Journal of Economics* 113(4):1169-1213. Retrieved May 9, 2015 (http://economics.mit.edu/files/563).

30. Autor, David H., Lawrence F. Katz and Melissa S. Kearney. 2006. "Measuring and Interpreting Trends in Economic Inequality." *AEA Papers and Proceedings* 96(2):189-194. Retrieved May 9, 2015 (http://economics.mit.edu/files/584). Card, David and John E. DiNardo. 2002. "Skill-Biased Technological Change and Rising Wage Inequality: Some Problems and Puzzles." *Journal of Labor Economics* 20(4):733-783. Retrieved May 9, 2015 (http://eml.berkeley.edu/~card/papers/skill-tech-change.pdf).

31. *Op. cit. Card, David and John E. DiNardo.*

32. *Op. cit. Bivens, Josh and Lawrence Mishel.*

33. Mishel, Lawrence, Josh Bivens, Elise Gould and Heidi Shierholz. 2012. "Appendices." *The State of Working America*, 12th Edition. Retrieved May 9, 2015 (http://stateofworkingamerica.org/files/book/Appendices.pdf).

34. Acemoglu, Daron. 2009. "When Does Labor Scarcity Encourage Innovation?" National Bureau of Economic Research Working Paper No. 14809. Retrieved May 9, 2015 (http://www.nber.org/papers/w14809.pdf).

35. Skott, Peter and Frederick Guy. 2007. "A Model of Power-Biased Technological Change." *Economics Letters* 95(1):124-131. Retrieved May 9, 2015 (http://www.sciencedirect.com/science/article/pii/S0165176506003363).

36. Acemoglu, Daron, David Autor, David Dorn and Gordon H. Hanson. 2014. "Import Competition and the Great U.S. Employment

Sag of the 2000s." National Bureau of Economic Research Working Paper No. 20395. Retrieved May 9, 2015 (http://economics.mit.edu/files/9811).

37. Autor, David H., David Dorn and Gordon H. Hanson. 2013. "The China Syndrome: Local Labor Market Effects of Import Competition in the United States." *American Economic Review* 103(6):2121-2168. Retrieved May 9, 2015 (http://economics.mit.edu/files/6613).

38. White, Roger. 2011. "Employment Effects of Increased Import Competition." Retrieved May 9, 2015 (http://citeseerx.ist.psu.edu/viewdoc/download?doi=10.1.1.198.4904&rep=rep1&type=pdf).

39. Stolper, W. F. and Paul A. Samuelson. 1941. "Protection and Real Wages." *Review of Economic Studies* 9(1):58–73. Lippoldt, Douglas, editor. *Policy Priorities for International Trade and Jobs.* International Collaborative Initiative on Trade and Employment, Organisation for Economic Co-ordination and Development. Retrieved May 9, 2015 (http://www.oecd.org/site/tadicite/50286917.pdf).

40. Feenstra, Robert C. and Gordon H. Hanson. 1996. "Globalization, Outsourcing, and Wage Inequality." *The American Economic Review* 86(2):240-245. Retrieved May 9, 2015 (https://ideas.repec.org/a/aea/aecrev/v86y1996i2p240-45.html). Elsby, Michael W.L., Bard Hobijn, and Aysegul Sahin. 2010. "The Labor Market in the Great Recession." *Brookings Papers on Economic Activity*, Spring 2010. Retrieved May 9, 2015 (http://www.brookings.edu/~/media/Projects/BPEA/Spring%202010/2010a_bpea_elsby.PDF). Blinder, Alan S. 2006. "Offshoring: The Next Industrial Revolution?" *Foreign Affairs*, March/April 2006 Issue. Retrieved May 9, 2015 (https://www.foreignaffairs.com/articles/2006-03-01/offshoring-next-industrial-revolution).

41. Authors' analysis of FRED civilian labor force level data. Federal Reserve Bank of St. Louis. 2015. "Civilian Labor Force Participation Rate." FRED Economic Data. Retrieved May 8, 2015 (http://research.stlouisfed.org/fred2/series/CIVPART).

42. *Op. cit. Stiglitz, Joseph E. "Intellectual Property Rights . . ."*